D0404129

Best Easy Day Hikes
San Jose

Help Us Keep This Guide Up to Date

Every effort has been made by the author and editors to make this guide as accurate and useful as possible. However, many things can change after a guide is published—trails are rerouted, regulations change, facilities come under new management, etc.

We would love to hear from you concerning your experiences with this guide and how you feel it could be improved and kept up to date. While we may not be able to respond to all comments and suggestions, we'll take them to heart and we'll also make certain to share them with the authors. Please send your comments and suggestions to the following address:

The Globe Pequot Press
Reader Response/Editorial Department
P.O. Box 480
Guilford, CT 06437

Or you may e-mail us at:

editorial@GlobePequot.com

Thanks for your input, and happy trails!

eries

Best Easy Day Hikes
San Jose

Tracy Salcedo-Chourré

FALCONGUIDES ®

GUILFORD, CONNECTICUT
HELENA, MONTANA

AN IMPRINT OF THE GLOBE PEQUOT PRESS

FALCONGUIDES®

Maps created by Offroute Inc. © Morris Book
Publishing, LLC

Library of Congress Cataloging-in-Publication
Data is available on file.

ISBN: 978-0-7627-5115-0

Printed in the United States of America

10 9 8 7 6 5 4 3 2 1

Contents

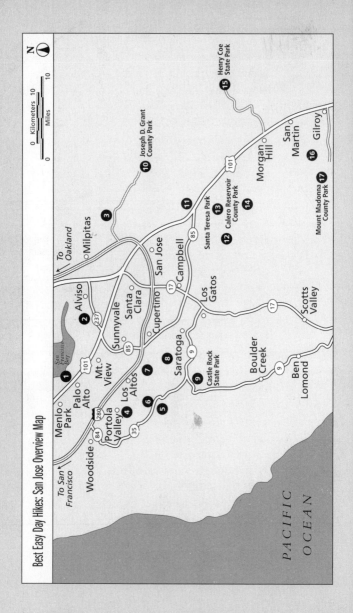

Best Easy Day Hikes: San Jose Overview Map

Acknowledgments

I am indebted to the many hikers and lovers of wildlands that have worked over the years to preserve parks and trails throughout the Bay Area. A guidebook like this wouldn't be possible without their efforts.

Thanks to the land managers who have taken the time to review the hikes described in this guide, and to guidebook authors who have shared their impressions of and experiences on San Francisco–area trails both in books and online. In particular I'd like to thank the following park officials for their input: communications specialist Leigh Ann Maze and other staff at Midpeninsula Regional Open Space District, public information officer Tamara Shear and other staff at Santa Clara County Parks, ranger John Verhoeven at Henry Coe State Park, ranger Miles Standish at Castle Rock State Park, and Yves Zsutty, trail network program manager with the city of San Jose.

Thanks to The Globe Pequot Press and its fine editors and production staff for inviting me to take on this project and helping me make it the best it can be.

Thanks also to family, friends, and neighbors who introduced me to Bay Area trails over the years and offered suggestions for this guide, including the Chourré clan, my parents Jesse and Judy Salcedo, brother Nick and his wife Nancy, brother Chris and his partner Angela Jones, and many others.

My husband, Martin, and sons Jesse, Cruz, and Penn, have been unfailing supporters of my work as a writer and teacher. I'm grateful and very lucky to share my journey with them.

Introduction

Looking down on the Santa Clara Valley from on high, the whirring and clicking of the computer industry that drives South Bay lifestyles drops away. Stand in a mossy forest of oaks and firs or in a whistling grassland and you won't remember deadlines, office politics, or the shower curtain that needs to be replaced at home. No, all you'll think about is your next wildland escape and which trail you'll take there.

A San Francisco native, I grew up surrounded by a natural beauty that is unique to the Bay Area—these landscapes are my foundation. Deep dark redwood groves, the smell of bay laurel on hot summer afternoons, bright fields of lupines, poppies, and golden grasses stretched over rolling hills . . . I've been very lucky.

Lucky, too, in that my job is to hike Bay Area trails and then write about them. The gift of guidebook writing was given to me by a publisher friend in Colorado who knew I loved the great outdoors—probably because I spent so much time gazing out the office window at the snowy summit of Mount Evans. After years writing guidebooks to Colorado's mountain trails, my husband and I returned to the North Bay to raise our children, and I started describing the hills and beaches and forests that inspired my love of nature in the first place.

Each hike in this guide is unique for its ecology, history, topography, or natural beauty. These routes serve as gateways to other trails; if the route described here doesn't fit your needs, you can be sure another in that park or a neighboring open-space preserve will.

From the highlands of Henry Coe State Park to the marshes of Palo Alto's Baylands, I hope you'll find these hikes as eye-opening and satisfying as I have.

The Nature of the Bay

Residents of the San Francisco Bay Area are almost universally outdoorsy. In the San Jose area interests range from the relatively easy (gardening) to relatively radical (hang gliding and rock climbing). Hiking strikes a middle ground, and this guide aims for that, showcasing relatively short routes that take trekkers into parks that protect bayside marshes, coastal mountaintops and ridges, oak woodlands, and former ranches.

Wherever you wander, knowing a few details about the nature of the South Bay will enhance your explorations.

Weather

The San Francisco Bay Area essentially has two seasons, dry and rainy. The rainy season generally runs from November through March, and includes rainstorms that can drop anywhere from a trace to several inches of rain. In the dry season, from April through October, very little rain falls, though fog can roll in off the Pacific at any time.

The San Jose area encompasses a couple of microclimates, bayside and inland. Along the bayshore, from Palo Alto to Alviso, maritime effects are more strongly felt, and the fog, if it rolls in, is more likely to linger. Temperatures are generally moderate, with daytime highs in winter in the 50s and 60s, and summer highs in the 70s and 80s.

Temperatures farther from the water, especially in the southern and eastern Santa Clara Valley along the U.S. Highway 101 corridor, are generally higher in summer, ranging from the 70s to the 90s. The occasional heat wave shoots the mercury above 100 degrees, but these are generally short-lived, as the bay's natural air conditioner—the fog—inevitably creeps back. Average daytime temperatures in winter range from the 50s to the high 60s, but the mercury can dip to freezing during cold snaps. Inland peaks like Mount Hamilton receive occasional snowfall as well.

Conditions on trails built on adobe (clay) soils can degenerate into boot-sucking mud after a heavy winter rain. A couple days of dry weather will harden up the surface enough for hikers to pass easily.

Critters

Most likely you'll encounter only benign, sweet creatures on these trails, such as deer, squirrels, rabbits, and a variety of songbirds and shorebirds.

But the South Bay's parklands are also habitat for mountain lions and rattlesnakes. Signs at trailheads warn hikers if these animals might be present. Encounters are infrequent, but you should familiarize yourself with the proper behavior should you run across either a dangerous snake or cat. Snakes generally only strike if they are threatened. Keep your distance and they will keep theirs. If you come across a cat, make yourself as big as possible and do not run. If you don't act like or look like prey, you stand a good chance of not being attacked.

Be Prepared

It would be tough to find a safer place for a hike than in the San Jose area. Still, hikers should be prepared, whether they are out for a short stroll along the waterfront in Alviso or headed to the rocky forests of Castle Rock State Park.

Some specific advice:

- Know the basics of first aid, including how to treat bleeding, bites and stings, and fractures, strains, or sprains. Pack a first-aid kit on each excursion.
- Be prepared for both heat and cold by dressing in layers.
- Carry a backpack in which you can store extra clothing, ample drinking water and food, and whatever goodies, like guidebooks, cameras, and binoculars, you might want.
- Many area trails have good cell phone coverage. Bring your device, but make sure you've turned it off or got it on the vibrate setting while hiking. Nothing like a "wake the dead"-loud ring to startle every creature, including fellow hikers.
- Keep children under careful watch. Children should carry a plastic whistle; if they become lost, they should stay in one place and blow the whistle to summon help.

Zero Impact

Trails in the San Jose area are heavily used year-round. We, as trail users and advocates, must be especially vigilant to make sure our passage leaves no lasting mark. Here are some basic guidelines for preserving trails in the region:

- Pack out all your own trash, including biodegradable items like orange peels. You might also pack out garbage left by less-considerate hikers.
- Don't approach or feed any wild creatures—the ground squirrel eyeing your snack food is best able to survive if it remains self-reliant.

- Don't pick wildflowers or gather rocks, antlers, feathers, and other treasures along the trail. Removing these items will only take away from the next hiker's backcountry experience.
- Avoid damaging trailside soils and plants by remaining on the established route. This is also a good rule of thumb for avoiding poison oak and stinging nettle, common regional trailside irritants.
- Don't cut switchbacks, which can promote erosion.
- Be courteous by not making loud noises while hiking.
- Many of these trails are multiuse, which means you'll share them with other hikers, trail runners, mountain bikers, and equestrians. Familiarize yourself with the proper trail etiquette, yielding the trail when appropriate.
- Use outhouses at trailheads or along the trail.

San Jose Boundaries and Corridors

For the purposes of this guide, San Jose–area hikes are contained within Santa Clara County (with the exception of Castle Rock State Park, which is just over the line in Santa Cruz County). The hikes are listed north to south from the Santa Clara County line in Palo Alto on the west side and in Milpitas on the east. All hikes are within an hour's drive of the San Jose city center.

Several major traffic arteries converge in San Jose. From the East Bay, Interstates 880 and 680 feed into the area, while from the San Francisco peninsula, Interstate 280 and US 101 funnel most traffic. The main highway south of San Jose into southern Santa Clara Valley is US 101. Directions to trailheads are given from one of these arteries.

For hikes north of the Santa Clara County line on the peninsula, check out *Best Easy Day Hikes San Francisco Peninsula*. Hikes north of the county line on the east side are described in *Best Easy Day Hikes San Francisco's East Bay*.

Land Management

The following government organizations and departments manage most of the public lands described in this guide, and can provide further information on these hikes and other trails in their service areas.

- California State Parks, Department of Parks and Recreation, 416 Ninth Street, Sacramento, CA 95814; P.O. Box 942896, Sacramento, CA 94296; (800) 777-0369 or (916) 653-6995; www.parks.ca.gov; info@parks.ca.gov. A complete listing of state parks, including those in the Bay Area, is available on the Web site, along with park brochures and maps.

- Santa Clara County Parks and Recreation Department, 298 Garden Hill Drive, Los Gatos, CA 95032-7699; (408) 355-2200; www.parkhere.org. Natural-surface trails in the parks may be temporarily closed to mountain bikers and equestrians during the winter months; call the trails hotline at (408) 355-2200 option 7 for current conditions.

- Midpeninsula Regional Open Space District, 330 Distel Circle, Los Altos, CA 94022-1404; (650) 691-1200; www.openspace.org; info@openspace.org. Open space parks dot the peninsula from south of the San Francisco city limits into Santa Clara County. Visit the Web site for specific park information and maps.

A number of regional trails run through the San Jose area, including the San Francisco Bay Trail (baytrail.abag.ca .gov), which follows the bayshore, and the Bay Area Ridge Trail (www.ridgetrail.org), which cruises ridgetops. Portions of these regional trails are incorporated into shorter routes in some of San Jose's parks.

Public Transportation

A number of bus, rail, and ferry services link communities in the San Francisco Bay Area. For general public transit information and links to specific transit sites, visit http://511.org or call 511 from anywhere in the San Francisco metropolitan area.

The Santa Clara Valley Transit Authority (VTA) provides bus, light rail, and shuttle services throughout the San Jose area. The address is 3331 North First Street, San Jose, CA 95134; (408) 321-2300; www.vta.org.

How to Use This Guide

This guide is designed to be simple and easy to use. Each hike is described with a map and summary information that delivers the trail's vital statistics including distance, difficulty, fees and permits, park hours, canine compatibility, and trail contacts. Directions to the trailhead are also provided, along with a general description of what you'll see along the way. A detailed route finder (Miles and Directions) sets forth mileages between significant landmarks along the trail.

Hike Selection

This guide describes trails that are accessible to every hiker, whether a visitor from out of town or someone lucky enough to live in the San Jose area. The hikes are no longer than 5 miles round-trip, and some are considerably shorter. They range in difficulty from short, flat excursions perfect for a family outing to more challenging treks through the hills and along ridgetops. While these trails are among the best, keep in mind that nearby trails, often in the same park or preserve, may offer options better suited to your needs. I've attempted to space hikes throughout the South Bay region so that wherever your starting point, you'll find a great easy day hike nearby.

Difficulty Ratings

These are all easy hikes, but easy is a relative term. Some would argue that no hike involving any kind of climbing is easy, but in the Bay Area hills are a fact of life. To aid in the selection of a hike that suits particular needs and abilities, each is rated easy, moderate, or more challenging. Bear in mind that even the most challenging hike can be made easy by hiking within your limits and taking rests when you need them.

- **Easy** hikes are generally short and flat, taking no longer than an hour to complete.
- **Moderate** hikes involve increased distance and relatively small changes in elevation, and will take one to two hours to complete.
- **More challenging** hikes feature some steep stretches and generally take longer than two hours to complete.

These are completely subjective ratings—keep in mind that what you think is easy is entirely dependent on your level of fitness and the adequacy of your gear (primarily shoes). If you are hiking with a group, you should select a hike with a rating that's appropriate for the least fit and prepared in your party.

Approximate hiking times are based on the assumption that on flat ground, most walkers average 2 miles per hour. Adjust that rate by the steepness of the terrain and your level of fitness (subtract time if you're an aerobic animal and add time if you're hiking with kids), and you have a ballpark hiking duration. Be sure to add more time if you plan to picnic or take part in other activities like bird watching or photography.

Trail Finder

Best Hikes for Beach/Coast Lovers

- 1 Baylands Trail (Palo Alto Baylands Park)
- 2 Alviso Slough Trail (Alviso Marina County Park)

Best Hikes for Children

- 3 Penitencia Creek Trail (Alum Rock Park)
- 16 Chitactac Adams Heritage County Park
- 17 Miller Ruins Loop (Mount Madonna County Park)

Best Hike for Dogs

- 10 Circle Corral and Bass Lake Loop (Joseph D. Grant County Park)

Best Hike for Peak Baggers

- 15 Top of the Ridge Tour (Henry Coe State Park)

Best Hikes for Great Views

- 1 Baylands Trail (Palo Alto Baylands Park)
- 13 Coyote Peak/Ridge Trail Loop (Santa Teresa County Park)
- 15 Top of the Ridge Tour (Henry Coe State Park)

Best Hikes for Nature Lovers

- 5 Stevens Creek Nature Trail (Monte Bello Open Space Preserve)
- 9 Castle Rock and Castle Rock Falls Tour (Castle Rock State Park)

Best Hikes for History Buffs

- 12 English Camp Loop (Almaden Quicksilver County Park)
- 16 Chitactac Adams Heritage County Park

Map Legend

══⟨90⟩══	Interstate Highway
══⟨30⟩══	U.S. Highway
══⟨20⟩══	State Highway
══⟨41⟩══	Local/Forest Roads
═ ═ ═ ═	Unimproved Road
- - - - -	Trail
▬▬▬▬▬	Featured Route
━━━━━	Paved Trail
─────	River/Creek
—··—··—	Intermittent Stream
▨▨▨	Golf Course
	Marsh/Swamp
	Local Park/Preserve
	State Park/County Park
‿	Bridge
⛺	Campground
❷	Information
⁑	Gate
🅿	Parking
▲	Peak
⛲	Picnic Area
■	Point of Interest
👫	Ranger Station
🚻	Restroom
≡	Steps
☎	Telephone
❻	Trailhead
彡	Waterfall
🔍	Viewpoint
🎒	Water

1 Baylands Trail (Palo Alto Baylands Park)

Meander through the domain of shorebirds and salt marshes on this scenic, lengthy stretch of trail along the bayshore.

Distance: 5.2 miles out and back

Approximate hiking time: 3 hours

Difficulty: Moderate

Trail surface: Flat, wide gravel trail

Best season: Year-round

Other trail users: Cyclists, trail runners

Canine compatibility: Leashed dogs permitted

Fees and permits: None

Schedule: Hours in Palo Alto open space parks vary with the season. In the summer months (early May to early September), the park opens at 8:00 a.m. and closes between 8:30 and 9:00 p.m. In spring and fall, hours are from 8:00 a.m. to 7:00 p.m. In winter (November through the end of February) the park is open from 8:00 a.m. until 5:30 or 6:00 p.m., depending on daylight hours. A complete list of hours available by visiting the city of Palo Alto's open space Web site at www.cityofpaloalto .org; follow the links for Arts, Parks, and Recreation.

Maps: USGS Mountain View; City of Palo Alto brochure and map

Trail contact: City of Palo Alto Open Space, 1305 Middlefield Road, Palo Alto, CA 94301; (650) 496-6962; www .cityofpaloalto.org/depts/csd/ parks_and_open_space/ preserves_and_open_spaces. You can also call (650) 617-3156.

Other: The Lucy Evans Baylands Nature Interpretive Center is at 2775 Embarcadero Road. The center is open Tuesday and Wednesday from 10:00 a.m. to 5:00 p.m., Thursday and Friday from 2:00 to 5:00 p.m., and Saturday and Sunday from 1:00 to 5:00 p.m.

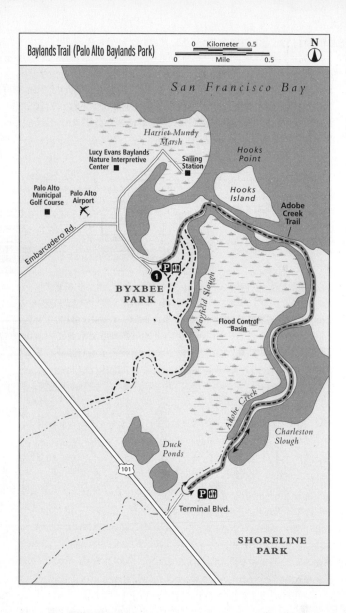

Baylands Trail (Palo Alto Baylands Park)

0 Kilometer 0.5

0 Mile 0.5

N

San Francisco Bay

Harriet Mundy Marsh

Hooks Point

Lucy Evans Baylands Nature Interpretive Center

Sailing Station

Hooks Island

Palo Alto Municipal Golf Course

Palo Alto Airport

Adobe Creek Trail

Embarcadero Rd.

1

BYXBEE PARK

Mayfield Slough

Flood Control Basin

Adobe Creek

Charleston Slough

Duck Ponds

101

Terminal Blvd.

SHORELINE PARK

Finding the trailhead: From U.S. Highway 101 in Palo Alto, take the Embarcadero Road exit. Head east on Embarcadero Road for 0.8 mile, past the Palo Alto Municipal Golf Course, to a T intersection. Turn right (southeast) on Embarcadero Road, continuing 1 mile to the end of the road at the Byxbee Park parking lot and trailhead. *DeLorme Northern California Atlas & Gazetteer:* Page 115 A4. GPS: N37 27.055' W122 06.391'.

The Hike

Amazingly, you'll feel completely separate from all that the South Bay is famous for—high tech, fast living, crowded freeways—on this stretch of trail, which thrusts you into the realm of shorebirds in an arguably pristine bayshore environment.

The trail begins in Byxbee Park, part of a network of bayshore parks stitched together along the San Francisco Bay Trail. The Byxbee trailhead hosts a trail map, trashcans, water, and restrooms. Set off to the right (east) on the Marsh Front Trail, which splits almost immediately. Stay left on the lower Adobe Creek Trail, a wide dirt track that leads into the marshland. Some interesting art installations, including a pole field, have been erected on the hillside to the right (southeast), and a number of trails branch off the main track into this area. Stay left on the lower track heading toward the bay, but keep an eye on the poles, as they make perfect perches for the local birdlife.

The landscape art is provocative and the views are beautiful, but it's the birds that enliven the route. Brilliantly white great and snowy egrets, great blue herons, perky-tailed ruddy ducks, western grebes with elegant necks, American white pelicans with orange clown feet, ubiquitous gulls—they ply the quiet waters of Mayfield and Charleston

Sloughs. This is also the domain of the northern harrier, a magnificent raptor with a distinctive white rump patch—a rare, thrilling sight.

Cross the slough gate at the half-mile mark, where you'll find benches that allow you to enjoy views over the bay. The path rides atop a levee that separates the slough from the open bay, curving in a long arc eastward, and then westward. Views are of the East Bay hills (through a net of power lines), with Hook Island in the foreground, and the dark foothills of the Santa Cruz Mountains to the west.

Pass a pond on your right as you leave Hook Island behind at 0.8 mile, and there is nothing but bay between you and Oakland. At 1.2 miles the trail curves slowly westward atop a levee that separates a narrow arm of the bay on the left (south) from Adobe Creek on the right (north).

A gate blocks access to another levee at 1.5 miles at a trail marker; and just beyond, an interpretive sign describes the interrelationship between different creatures in the tidal system. The trail now meanders between Charleston Slough and Adobe Creek, where sandpipers pick at the mudflats for a meal.

Pass an interpretive sign on biodiversity as civilization becomes more prominent ahead; at 2.5 miles you'll reach a trail intersection with routes to Shoreline Lake (left/east) and the paved San Francisco Bay Trail (right/northwest) at the edge of Coast Casey Forebay. A map of Stevens Creek and Shoreline Park is on the back of the power station at the trail junction. Restrooms and benches lie 0.1 mile ahead at the Terminal Boulevard/Adobe Creek trailhead, where you'll also find parking. Return as you came.

Options: A number of trails lace through the greater Baylands and adjacent Shoreline Park. You can visit the duck point, nature center, picnic areas, and sailing station by heading northeast on Embarcadero Road from Byxbee Park.

Miles and Directions

0.0 Start on the Marsh Front Trail. At the trail fork, stay left on the Adobe Creek Trail.

0.2 Pass several smaller trails to the right, leading up into the Byxbee Park Hills. Stay left on the Adobe Creek Trail.

0.3 Pass the pole field and reach a trail marker denoting the Adobe Creek Trail. Again, stay left (east), heading toward Shoreline Lake and away from the pole field and the Renzel Wetlands area.

0.5 The trail bends southeast and crosses the Mayfield Slough gate.

0.8 Pass side trails that skirt a pond, which can be dry in late season.

1.2 The trail bends west, with Adobe Creek on the right.

1.5 Pass a gated levee, a trail marker, and an interpretive sign.

2.4 Pass another interpretive sign.

2.5 Reach the junction with the trail to Shoreline Lake on the left (southeast) and the paved San Francisco Bay Trail on the right (northwest). Continue straight on the trail to the restrooms at the Terminal Boulevard trailhead.

2.6 Arrive at Terminal Boulevard. Return as you came.

5.2 Arrive back at the Byxbee Park trailhead and parking area.

2 Alviso Slough Trail (Alviso Marina County Park)

Boardwalks and easy levee-top walking lead out through marshlands to the bayshore, where you'll enjoy fantastic bay views and birding opportunities.

Distance: 2.8 miles out and back

Approximate hiking time: 1.5 hours

Difficulty: Easy

Trail surface: Dirt trail tread, boardwalks

Best season: Year-round. Winter winds, high surf, and rain may render the trail impassable.

Other trail users: Cyclists, trail runners

Canine compatibility: No dogs permitted

Fees and permits: None

Schedule: The park is open from 8:00 a.m. to sunset daily. Trail access is from sunrise to sunset; if the gates are closed, park legally on the street.

Maps: USGS Milpitas; Santa Clara County Park brochure and map to the park available at the trailhead and online

Trail contact: Santa Clara County Parks and Recreation Department, 298 Garden Hill Drive, Los Gatos, CA 95032-7699; (408) 355-2200; www .parkhere.org

Special considerations: Bring binoculars, a camera, and a field guide if you are interested in identifying the many birds you'll see in the marsh and along the shoreline.

Other: You'll find restrooms, infor-mation, picnic tables, and water at the trailhead. The trail is part of the San Francisco Bay Trail.

Finding the trailhead: From U.S. Highway 101 in San Jose, take Interstate 880 north (toward Oakland) to the Highway 237 exit. Head west on Highway 237 toward Mountain View. Stay on Highway 237 for 1.9 miles to the North First Street exit. Follow North First Street

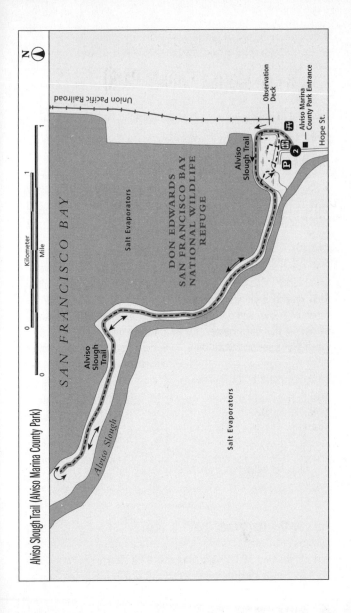

Alviso Slough Trail (Alviso Marina County Park)

SAN FRANCISCO BAY

Union Pacific Railroad

Alviso Slough

Alviso Slough Trail

Alviso Slough Trail

Salt Evaporators

DON EDWARDS
SAN FRANCISCO
BAY NATIONAL
WILDLIFE
REFUGE

Salt Evaporators

Observation Deck

Alviso Marina
County Park Entrance

Hope St.

Kilometer

Mile

N

(which becomes Taylor) for 0.9 mile to Liberty Street. Turn right on Liberty Street and go 1 block to Catherine Street. Turn left on Catherine Street and follow it for 0.2 mile to unsigned Hope Street. Turn right (north) on Hope Street and follow it to its end at the park. The trailhead is in the east end of the parking lot near the restroom. *DeLorme Northern California Atlas & Gazetteer:* Page 115 A5. GPS: N37 25.793' W121 58.750'.

The Hike

Snowy egrets rise like shooting stars out of the reeds and rushes that surround Alviso Slough. They have plenty of company, with other shorebirds cruising low over the water looking for a meal, and still others poking in the mud at low tide for the tasty nuggets that hide below the surface.

The birds—and the hikers who enjoy their company—reap benefits proffered by the slough's proximity to the Don Edwards San Francisco Bay National Wildlife Refuge, which preserves about 30,000 acres of water and tidal lands in the South and East Bays. Under the auspices of the refuge, the bay's once-expansive marshlands, many of which were put to use as salt evaporation ponds and in other commercial enterprises, have been reclaimed as habitat for wildlife, including both migratory and resident ducks, gulls, songbirds, and raptors. It's paradise for the winged, and for the wingless who love to watch them.

The levee-top trail offers more than just bird watching to visitors. The wide flat path, perfect for families and hardy wheelchair users, stretches beyond the boundaries of the county park as part of the regional San Francisco Bay Trail. It also offers unobstructed views of the San Francisco peninsula and Santa Cruz Mountains to the west, and the hills of the East Bay.

Once part of the domain of the Ohlone people, the Alviso marina and slough take their names from Ignacio Alviso, a member of Juan Bautista de Anza's 1776 expedition into Alta California. The area became part of Alviso's *rancho,* Rincon de los Esteros, and shipping from the site began with hides and tallow from the ranch. Later, according to park literature, quicksilver (mercury) from the nearby New Almaden mine was shipped from the site, which evolved into a shipping and transportation hub. Interpretive signs at the trailhead illustrate the development that took place at the Port of Alviso. The vagaries of nature and enterprise conspired in the demise of the port: The site was repeatedly flooded when nearby streams and the Guadalupe River overflowed their banks, and business dried up when the railroad bypassed the site.

The track is easy and straightforward, following the levees around the restored marsh at the heart of the county park, then extending north and west up the bayshore on the San Francisco Bay Trail. It's described here as a 2.8-mile trek, but it can be lengthened or shortened to meet any hiker's needs.

Miles and Directions

0.0 Start by heading east from the restrooms through the picnic area and past the gate. The trail is gravel beyond the gate and overlooks railroad tracks and a salt pond, with East Bay hills rising in the distance.

0.1 Arrive at an observation deck with benches and interpretive signs describing the creatures, from worms to mice, that inhabit the marshlands. At the junction with the eastward extension of San Francisco Bay Trail and Anza Trail, go left (west) on the Alviso Slough Trail.

0.3 Pass a boardwalk on the left (south) that you'll use on the return leg of the hike. An interpretive sign on salt ponds is at this junction. Stay straight (briefly southwest, then northwest) on the Alviso Slough Trail.

0.5 The trail heads north with the slough on the left (west) and open water on the right (east). Great views surround you, across the blue-green water to Mission and Monument Peaks in the east and across the marshes west to the blue-gray rampart of the Santa Cruz Mountains.

1.0 Pass the 1-mile marker. A derelict wooden boat sails the reeds alongside the slough on the left (west).

1.5 The trail reaches a levee junction and the turnaround point. The jumbled levee to the right (east) is closed, but you can turn left (west) to continue on the San Francisco Bay Trail. Otherwise, return as you came.

2.7 Arrive back at the junction with the boardwalk in the county park. Turn right (south) and pass through the "door" into the marsh. An interpretive sign describes the different plants that survive in the inhospitable wetland environments, including cord grass and salt grass.

2.8 Reach wedding-cake–tiered benches that climb back to the parking lot. Turn left (east) and follow the trail below the lot to the staircase that leads up to the trailhead.

3 Penitencia Creek Trail (Alum Rock Park)

History, health, and hiking merge on the flat track that follows Penitencia Creek from the grottos and pools of a one-time spa into a backcountry lush with sycamores, bigleaf maples, and oaks.

Distance: 1.4-mile lollipop
Approximate hiking time: 1 hour
Difficulty: Easy
Trail surface: Pavement, dirt roadway
Best season: Year-round, though both fall and spring are enhanced by the colors of changing foliage and wildflowers, respectively.
Other trail users: Trail runners, mountain bikers
Canine compatibility: No dogs permitted
Fees and permits: A $6 day use fee is charged on Saturday, Sunday, and holidays.
Schedule: The park is open from 8:00 a.m. to a half hour after sunset daily.
Maps: USGS Calaveras Reservoir; Alum Rock park map and brochure available at the park's visitor center

Trail contact: San Jose Department of Parks, Recreation and Neighborhood Services, 16240 Alum Rock Avenue, San Jose, CA 95127-1307; (408) 259-5477; www.sanjoseparks.org
Special considerations: When you reach the confluence of Penitencia and Aguague Creeks at the end of this route, you'll have entered mountain lion country. Proceed with caution and common sense.
Other: There are no trailhead amenities other than parking and an information board. Visitor center amenities include restrooms, water, information, picnic sites, playing greens, a volleyball court, and a pair of tot lots. Should you choose to start your hike at the visitor center, add 0.4 mile to your total hiking distance.

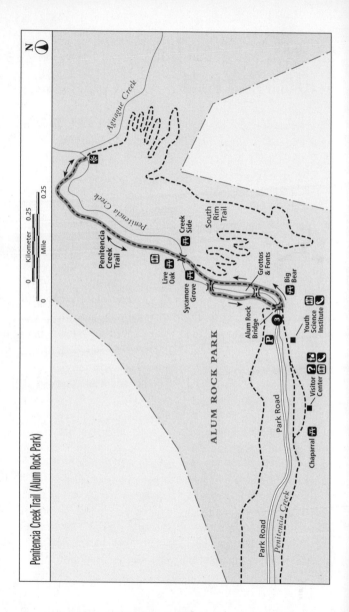

Penitencia Creek Trail (Alum Rock Park)

Finding the trailhead: From Interstate 680 in San Jose, take the McKee Road exit. Go west on McKee Road for 1 mile to North White Road. Turn left (north) on North White Road for 1.2 miles to Penitencia Creek Road. Turn right (west) on Penitencia Creek Road and go 0.7 mile to the park's entrance station. The trailhead is at the end of the last parking lot, 1.9 miles from the entrance station at the historic Alum Rock bridge. *DeLorme Northern California Atlas & Gazetteer:* Page 115 B7. GPS: N37 23.827' N121 47.878'.

The Hike

Tucked in a steep canyon in the hills east of downtown San Jose, Alum Rock Park has been a retreat for the city-weary since 1872. Its mineral springs, still collecting in grottos and fonts along the Penitencia Creek Trail, earned a spa located here national renown at the turn of the twentieth century. More than twenty springs contain seven different minerals including soda, magnesia, iron, and—you can smell this from the trail—sulphur. You can't "take the waters" these days, but you can enjoy their legacy along this short route.

The park's resort days ran from 1890 to the early 1930s. For two bits, you could ride a steam train run by the San Jose and Alum Rock Railroad to the spa and its baths, dance pavilion, and tearoom. Apparently, riding up to the resort wasn't too bad, but the open cars behind the "steam dummies," or engines, frequently jumped the tracks on the ride back down into town. For those with delicate constitutions, the ride no doubt jangled nerves they'd relaxed in the baths. Remnants of the railroad (later an electric line) include concrete abutments that once supported the tracks and an old trestle near Alum Rock.

From the trailhead at the Alum Rock bridge, the Penitencia Creek Trail is paved for a distance, passing a number of stone grottos and pools colored and scented with minerals. A dirt track on the opposite side of the creek weaves around these spa remnants, offering a more challenging walk for those interested. Picnic areas shelter beneath a forest of buckeye, maple, walnut, oak, and alder, all nurtured by the year-round flow of Penitencia Creek.

Farther east the steep-walled Penitencia Creek canyon narrows, the pavement ends, and the atmosphere of the trail becomes more natural and rustic. Sycamores and maples provide ample shade in summer, drop orange and yellow leaves in fall, and harbor noisy colonies of jays. The rocky creekbed is filled with trickling pools, even at the end of the dry season. By the time you reach the overlook at the confluence of Penitencia and Aguague Creeks, the turnaround point, you'll be fully immersed in a thick forest that harbors no hint of the storied pools that lie just downstream.

Options: Continue west on the Penitencia Creek Trail to explore more developed sections of the park, following a rail trail that lies on the bed of the former steam and electric rail line. The trail offers access to the Youth Science Institute and the park's visitor center, which is surrounded by playing greens, two tot lots, picnic areas and barbecues, and a sand volleyball court. Beyond the trail follows the creek west to the trestle over Alum Rock Road and the Rustic Lands and Quail Hollow picnic areas (about 1.1 mile from the Alum Rock bridge trailhead). The trail continues to the park's Penitencia Creek Road entrance.

Miles and Directions

0.0 Start by crossing the Alum Rock bridge and heading left (east) on the paved Penitencia Creek Trail. Stone bridges span Penitencia Creek, linking grottos and fonts on either side of the waterway. Remain on the paved route; the dirt trail option is described as part of the return route. Trailside interpretive signs describe the park's springs.

0.2 Reach the Sycamore Grove picnic area, with a phone, barbecues, trashcans, and a horseshoe pit. The South Rim Trail takes off to the right (south). Stay straight on the paved Penitencia Creek Trail.

0.3 Pass the Creek Side picnic area and cross a bridge. The Live Oak picnic area is up the stairs to the left (north). Stone cairns line the paved trail.

0.4 The pavement ends. Continue on the dirt track past Sachi's Rest picnic area.

0.7 Wind southward to a bridge that spans the narrow canyon floor and Penitencia Creek at the junction with the South Rim Trail. Cross the bridge (note that the abutment on the south side is built into a crotch in a huge old sycamore) and arrive at an overlook with benches at the confluence of Penitencia and Aguague Creeks. Turn around here and retrace your steps toward the trailhead.

1.2 On the west side of the Sycamore Grove picnic area, turn right and cross the bridge onto the north side of Penitencia Creek. A narrow dirt track skirts the creek, requiring some grotto-hopping, stair-climbing, pool-gazing, and little lizard-scaring.

1.4 Arrive back at the trailhead, passing an interpretive sign that describes the role earthquakes and volcanoes played in the formation of the park.

4 Sausal Pond Loop (Windy Hill Open Space Preserve)

Wildflowers and wild ducks top the list of highlights along this lovely loop, which also encompasses a sultry oak woodland and pleasant views of the surrounding hills and valleys.

Distance: 1.4-mile loop
Approximate hiking time: 1 hour
Difficulty: Moderate
Trail surface: Dirt singletrack and dirt road
Best season: Spring and fall. The trail can be sticky and muddy in the days following a winter rain.
Other trail users: Trail runners and equestrians on the Betsy Crowder Trail; cyclists, equestrians, and runners on the Sausal Pond Trail. The Betsy Crowder Trail is closed to horses when conditions are too wet.
Canine compatibility: Leashed dogs permitted on this trail loop. They are prohibited on other park trails, including the Razorback Ridge, Eagle, and Lost Trails.
Fees and permits: None
Schedule: The park is open from dawn to a half hour before sunset daily.

Maps: USGS Mindego Hill; map and brochure published by the Midpeninsula Regional Open Space District available at the park entrance and online
Trail contact: Midpeninsula Regional Open Space District, 330 Distel Circle, Los Altos, CA 94022-1404; (650) 691-1200; www.openspace.org
Special considerations: Mountain lions and rattlesnakes reside in these hills, so use caution and common sense when hiking in the preserve. Remain on trails to avoid contact with poison oak. Sudden oak death is present in the park, so take care to clear dirt and mud from your shoes to avoid spreading the contagion that has killed numerous oak trees in northern California.
Other: Trailhead amenities include parking, a vault toilet, and an information board.

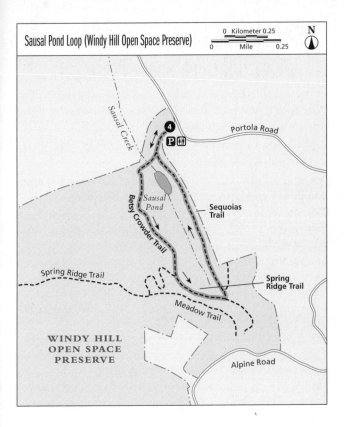

Finding the trailhead: From Interstate 280 in Palo Alto, north of San Jose, take the Alpine Road exit. Go southwest on Alpine Road for 3 miles to Portola Road and turn right (northwest). Follow Portola Road for 1 mile to the preserve entrance and parking lot on the left (west). The trailhead is at the west end of the dirt parking area near the restrooms. *DeLorme Northern California Atlas & Gazetteer:* Page 114 B3. GPS: N37 22.502' W122 13.418'.

The Hike

The summit of Windy Hill is touted as a great place to take in views of San Francisco Bay—and a great place to fly a kite or launch a hang glider (if you have the proper permit). But the park's lower reaches harbor a pond and oak woodland that are equally worthy of a hiker's attention.

The Betsy Crowder Trail, named for a one-time director on the Midpeninsula Regional Open Space District board, is a beautiful path through oaks and bays that rings with bird calls. In the rainy season moss on the trees swells with moisture, ferns send up new fronds and plump those that survived the long dry summer, and lacy lichens drip from branches overhead. This iridescent greenness filters the sun and insulates hikers from everything bright and harsh. On a weekday it can be so still in these woods that you may encounter deer or coyotes on the trail. Stop and watch: They may try to stare you down, but they'll eventually move on.

The trail climbs into an equally lovely meadowland, where wildflowers bloom through spring and early summer, and views open of the hills to the east and west. A bench dedicated to the trail's namesake offers the perfect rest stop.

The downhill leg of the loop follows the Spring Ridge Trail, a dirt road, through meadows and past remnants of the park's ranching history, including lichen-crusted split-rail fencing and a rickety chute that empties onto the edge of the trail.

Sausal Pond, shielded by a thick riparian curtain, is a protected area that serves as habitat for native and migratory birds. A short path at the spillway end of the pond leads to the shoreline, where you can watch for wood ducks, mallards, and green herons, among other species. Much like the woodland, the pond is quieting, despite its proximity to an apartment complex just across the trail. No fishing is permitted, and avoid disturbing the reed- and willow-choked banks, which are protected habitat.

Options: The Anniversary Trail, a 0.7-mile loop for hikers only on the west side of the park, offers great views, as do some of the longer trails in the 1,312-acre preserve.

Miles and Directions

0.0 Start by climbing the paved path west of the informational kiosk into chaparral.

0.1 At the trail intersection go right (west) on the Betsy Crowder Trail. A dedication sign is beyond the gate.

0.2 Switchback upward through a drainage.

0.5 Reach the Betsy Crowder bench in the meadow and enjoy the views.

0.6 Pass through a gate to the intersection with the Spring Ridge Trail. Turn left (east) on Spring Ridge Trail, which you'll share with cyclists. Ignore side trails as you descend.

0.7 At the trail intersection, head left (north) on the unnamed trail/dirt road that leads to Sausal Pond. Pass the Sequoias Trail, which goes right (east).

0.8 Pass a lichen-covered wooden chute, then descend along the Sausal Creek corridor. The trail is bordered on the left (west) by the creek and on the right (east) by a fence marking the property line. The Sequoias apartment complex is on the other side of the fence.

1.2 Pass the pond, which is screened by reeds and willows on the left (west) side of the trail. A social path at the north end, near the spillway, offers limited access for bird watchers, photographers, and other visitors.

1.3 Finish the descent at the junction with the Betsy Crowder Trail. Turn right (east) and retrace your steps toward the parking lot.

1.4 Arrive back at the trailhead.

5 Stevens Creek Nature Trail (Monte Bello Open Space Preserve)

A trek along the headwaters of Stevens Creek enfolds hikers in a deepening riparian habitat. Above, on the slopes of Black Mountain, wildflowers, raptors, and views dominate the scene.

Distance: 2.8-mile lollipop

Approximate hiking time: 2 hours

Difficulty: More challenging due to trail length and a steady descent and ascent

Trail surface: Dirt singletrack, dirt road

Best season: Spring and fall. Winter rains may render the trails muddy.

Other trail users: Hikers only on the Stevens Creek Nature Trail; cyclists, trail runners, and equestrians on the Canyon Trail

Canine compatibility: Dogs not permitted

Fees and permits: None

Schedule: The park is open from dawn to a half hour past sunset daily.

Maps: USGS Mindego Hill; South Skyline Region park map available at the trailhead (showing all the contiguous county and state open space preserves in the area), and the map and brochure published by the Midpeninsula Regional Open Space District available online

Trail contact: Midpeninsula Regional Open Space District, 330 Distel Circle, Los Altos, CA 94022-1404; (650) 691-1200; www.openspace.org

Special considerations: Mountain lions and rattlesnakes call the park home. While an encounter is unlikely, use caution and common sense when hiking. The park also hosts sudden oak death syndrome, which has killed a large number of oaks in northern California. Use brushes at the trailhead to clean your boots of possible contagion.

Other: You will find vault toilets, an information board, and lots of parking at the trailhead.

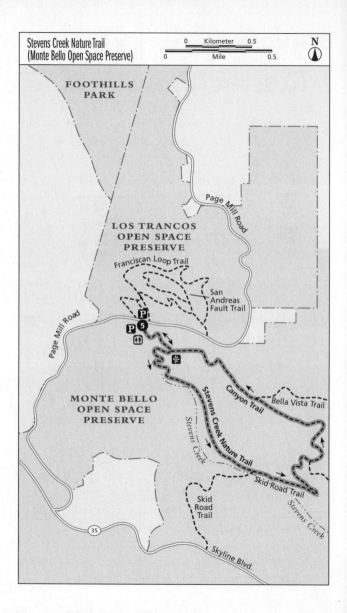

Stevens Creek Nature Trail
(Monte Bello Open Space Preserve)

FOOTHILLS PARK

Page Mill Road

LOS TRANCOS OPEN SPACE PRESERVE

Franciscan Loop Trail

San Andreas Fault Trail

Page Mill Road

MONTE BELLO OPEN SPACE PRESERVE

Canyon Trail

Bella Vista Trail

Stevens Creek Nature Trail

Stevens Creek

Skid-Road Trail

Skid Road Trail

Stevens Creek

35

Skyline Blvd.

N

0   Kilometer   0.5
0   Mile   0.5

Finding the trailhead: From Interstate 280 in Los Altos Hills, north of San Jose, take the Page Mill Road exit. Head west on Page Mill Road for 7.3 miles to the park entrance on the left (west) side of the narrow, winding, scenic road. *DeLorme Northern California Atlas & Gazetteer:* Page 115 B4. GPS: N37 19.514' W122 10.723'.

The Hike

Literature for Monte Bello Open Space Preserve swells with superlatives, touting the views from highland meadows as "incredible" and the riparian corridor that cradles the headwaters of Stevens Creek as "one of the finest in the Santa Cruz Mountains."

That about sums it up. It wasn't named "beautiful mountain" (in Italian) for nothing . . . .

At more than 2,000 feet in elevation, views south and west from the ridge where this loop trail begins are amazing. They stretch south past Black Mountain to dark Mount Umunhum, with its odd square topper of a building, and Loma Prieta, namesake of the epicenter of the earthquake that rattled the Bay Area in 1989. Westward the Stevens Creek drainage (which follows the San Andreas fault line) drops into a thick cover of oaks, bay laurels, and bigleaf maples, then is lost in the maze of forested canyons that converge in this part of the range.

In Stevens Creek Canyon the trail follows the evolving stream, which cascades through a cool, sun-dappled woodland supporting all the riparian wildlife and plant life you'd expect. In the rainy season ferns and mosses pop from the understory, and fragile California newts ramble across the trail. In summer the forest provides a cool haven for songbirds, lizards, and larger creatures like hikers. Interpretive signs along the trail provide insight into what you might see along the way.

The Canyon Trail offers a sunny ascent out of the canyon and into the grasslands, where wildflowers bloom in succession from late winter to early summer. The annual rye, oat, and rattlesnake grasses, inadvertently brought to California by Spanish explorers, overwhelmed native grasses that stayed green year-round; in modern times, these hills are green only for the duration of the rainy season, then dry to a distinctive crispy gold. They were fodder for cattle when the parklands were rangelands in the nineteenth and twentieth centuries, and now support deer and provide cover for ground squirrels, protecting them from the animals and raptors that prey on them.

Miles and Directions

0.0 Start at the trailhead near the information signboard in the southwest corner of the parking lot..

0.1 Descend through the grasses to a vista point at a trail junction, where an interpretive sign describes the high points on the southern and western horizon. Turn right (north) on the Stevens Creek Nature Trail.

0.3 Switchback down the open slope to an interpretive sign about bobcats.

0.4 Enter the shady Stevens Creek drainage. In late season, the creekbed may be dry.

0.5 Another set of switchbacks drops to a sign about poison oak. As you descend, the stream gathers speed and volume.

0.7 Switchbacks and a number of side-stream crossings drop to an interpretive sign that describes the ecology of "edges" at a patch of grassland.

0.8 The next set of switchbacks deposits you at a bridge near the confluence of Stevens Creek and a feeder stream. Beyond the descent mellows and the trail affords views of a more robust creek that flows around oxbow bends and through deep pools.

1.1 Pass a sign about the FBI (fungus, bacteria, and insects) that help decompose dead matter in the forest. A trail marker is not far beyond. Stairs lead to a creek crossing where you'll have to do some rock and root hopping to keep your boots dry.

1.2 Climb past interpretive signs about newts and western fence lizards (also called bluebellies) to the junction with the Skid Road Trail. Turn left (south) on the Skid Road/Stevens Creek Nature Trail toward the Canyon Trail.

1.7 After passing a few more interpretive signs and beginning the long climb out of the creek drainage, pass through a gate.

1.8 Arrive at the junction with the Canyon Trail. An interpretive sign describes the food chain. Turn left (northeast) on the Canyon Trail.

2.0 Pass a mile marker. Views open as you break out of the woods into the grasslands.

2.1 Pass a bench at a social trail, an interpretive sign about coyotes, then the junction with the Bella Vista Trail. Stay straight (up) on the wide Canyon Trail, then straight (up and north) again at the next junction.

2.4 Pass a sag pond on the right (east) and an interpretive sign that describes its formation and evolution. The junction with the singletrack leading to the Monte Bello parking area is just beyond. Turn left (up and northwest) on the singletrack.

2.5 Another trail junction: Go right (northwest) on the trail to the Monte Bello trailhead. Another junction follows; stay left (northwest) here.

2.7 Reach the trail junction at the vista point. Retrace your steps from here.

2.8 Arrive at the parking lot and trailhead.

6 San Andreas Fault Trail (Los Trancos Open Space Preserve)

In 1906 the San Andreas Fault ruptured, rocking the San Francisco Bay Area and forever altering perceptions of the seemingly serene landscapes. This hike loops through a woodland that sits atop the fault line, where interpretive markers offer insight into the impact of the quake.

Distance: 1.5-mile lollipop
Approximate hiking time: 1 hour
Difficulty: Easy
Trail surface: Dirt singletrack
Best season: Year-round. The trail may be muddy after a winter rain.
Other trail users: None
Canine compatibility: Dogs not permitted
Fees and permits: None
Schedule: The park is open from dawn until a half hour before sunset daily.
Maps: USGS Mindego Hill; San Andreas Fault Trail map and brochure published by the Midpeninsula Regional Open Space District available at the park and online; South Skyline Region park map available at the trailhead (showing all the contiguous open space parks and preserves in the area)
Trail contact: Midpeninsula

Regional Open Space District, 330 Distel Circle, Los Altos, CA 94022-1404; (650) 691-1200; www .openspace.org
Special considerations: Mountain lions and rattlesnakes inhabit these hills. While an encounter is unlikely, use care and caution when hiking in the area. The parklands also host sudden oak death syndrome, a disease that has killed a large number of oaks in northern California. Use shoe brushes at the trailheads to clean your boots of possible contagion.
Other: The parking lot at Los Trancos holds about twenty cars. There is also an information board at the trailhead. Vault toilets, another information board, and lots of parking are across Page Mill Road at neighboring Monte Bello Open Space Preserve.

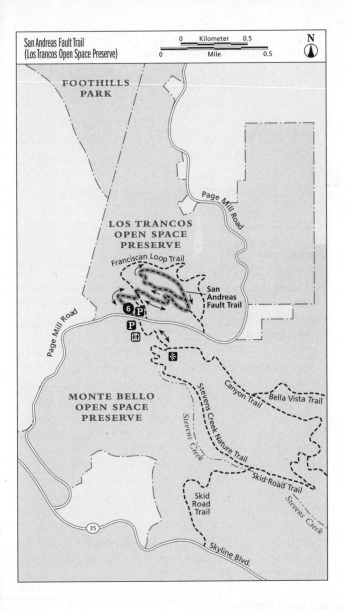

San Andreas Fault Trail
(Los Trancos Open Space Preserve)

0   Kilometer   0.5

0   Mile   0.5

N

FOOTHILLS
PARK

Page Mill Road

LOS TRANCOS
OPEN SPACE
PRESERVE

Franciscan Loop Trail

San
Andreas
Fault Trail

6 P

P

Page Mill Road

MONTE BELLO
OPEN SPACE
PRESERVE

Canyon Trail

Bella Vista Trail

Stevens Creek Nature Trail

Stevens Creek

Skid Road Trail

Stevens Creek

Skid
Road
Trail

35

Skyline Blvd.

Finding the trailhead: From Interstate 280 in Los Altos Hills north of San Jose, take the Page Mill Road exit. Head west on Page Mill Road for 7.3 miles to the park entrance on the right (east) side of the narrow, winding, scenic road. *DeLorme Northern California Atlas & Gazetteer:* Page 115 B4. GPS: N37 19.566' W122 10.788.'

The Hike

Ask for a defining historical event in San Francisco and the 1906 earthquake lurches to the forefront. The San Andreas Fault, source of the temblor, slices through the Bay Area and is the focus of this scenic interpretive trail.

Without the interpretive guide, available online and at the trailhead, many of the features along the trail that illustrate the impact of the 1906 quake might be overlooked. A few are obvious—yellow-topped posts that mark the San Andreas Fault itself, white-topped posts that mark smaller fault breaks, and a fence installed to show how much the land shifted in the 1906 event.

But with the guide, you'll be directed to more subtle changes that hint at the volatility that lies below the surface. The sag ponds near the trailhead and in the woodland, which fill with water in the rainy season, are depressions formed when the land was stretched and then subsided. Boulders on the hillside at the trailhead came from a mountain more than 23 miles away. Thick copses of willow thrive in areas moistened by springs, common in earthquake zones. Oak trees with limbs that grow parallel to the ground before reaching toward the sky may have toppled in the 1906 quake, but survived to send up new, unusual growth.

While the main draw may be earthquake-driven, the route has more to recommend it. From high points near the trailhead, views open over the bay north toward San Francisco and east toward Mount Diablo and the East Bay hills. On the wooded slopes along the lollipop portion of the trail, oaks, bay laurels, and pines conspire to create a pocket of peaceful woodland.

The beginning and end of the trail are close to Page Mill Road, which can be noisy on busy weekends. But in the forested hollow along the loop portion of the fault trail, no noise penetrates.

Miles and Directions

0.0 Start at the north end of the parking lot. A rocky climb up singletrack leads to interpretive marker 1 and great views of the bay.

0.1 Pass a second viewpoint, marker 2, and a bench dedicated to Stanley Morton, a founder of the Midpeninsula Regional Open Space District. Drop a few feet to a trail marker and follow the trail into the dense chaparral.

0.2 Trail intersections follow in quick succession. At the first go left (northeast) toward the bay. At the next go straight (east) on the signed FAULT trail.

0.3 Switchback down into oak and scrub that chatter with birds and squirrels. Another switchback keeps you on a downhill run.

0.4 At the intersection with the Franciscan Loop Trail and marker 3 go left (north) on the signed FAULT trail. A bench dedicated to Flora Lamson Hewlett marks the spot. The trail descends past a displaced fence line (marker 4), then marker 5. Look to the left to see a piece of wheeled machinery being consumed by the wilderness.

0.5 At the sign the trail splits; go left (northeast) on the lollipop loop.

0.6 Pass marker 6 at a grand old oak. Switchbacks lead down into the woodland, where fault markers glow white and yellow against a green backdrop.

0.9 Climb gently back to the start of the loop. Retrace your steps to the trailhead, heading right (uphill) at the junction with Franciscan Loop Trail.

1.4 At the intersection below the parking lot, which is visible to the left (west), you can either continue on the Fault trail retracing your steps to the trailhead, or turn left and climb directly to the parking area.

1.5 Arrive back at the trailhead and parking lot.

7 Coyote and Wildcat Loop Trails (Rancho San Antonio Open Space Preserve and County Park)

Well-maintained, moderately graded, and very popular, these trails lead to a lovely riparian corridor along Wildcat Creek and past picturesque Deer Hollow Farm.

Distance: 3.4-mile lollipop

Approximate hiking time: 2 hours

Difficulty: More challenging due to distance and moderate slopes

Trail surface: Pavement, natural dirt roads, natural dirt singletrack

Best season: Spring, summer, and fall. The Coyote Trail can be sticky and muddy for a couple of days following a winter rain.

Other trail users: Trail runners (lots of them); equestrians on the Coyote Trail; cyclists on the Lower Meadow Trail from Deer Hollow Farm to the trailhead

Canine compatibility: Dogs not permitted

Fees and permits: None

Schedule: The county park and open space preserve are open from dawn to a half hour after sunset daily.

Maps: USGS Cupertino; an open space and county park map published online at both the Mid-peninsula Regional Open Space District and Santa Clara County Parks Web sites. A map of the combined parks is available at the information kiosk at the park boundary at the north end of the North Meadow.

Trail contact: Midpeninsula Regional Open Space District, 330 Distel Circle, Los Altos, CA 94022-1404; (650) 691-1200; www.openspace.org. Santa Clara County Parks and Recreation Department, 298 Garden Hill Drive, Los Gatos, CA 95032-7699; (408) 355-2200; www .parkhere.org.

Special considerations: The park is habitat for mountain lions, rattlesnakes, ticks, and

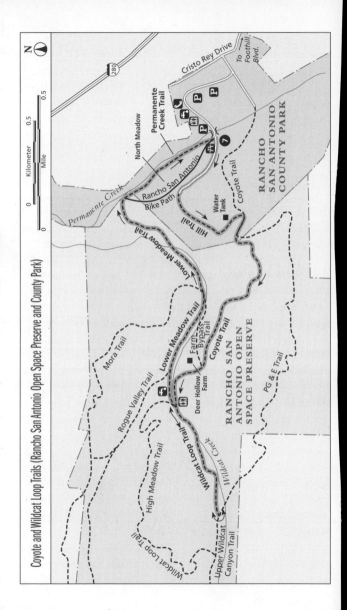

Coyote and Wildcat Loop Trails (Rancho San Antonio Open Space Preserve and County Park)

poison oak. Remain on trails to avoid contact with ticks and poison oak; use caution and common sense in the unlikely event that you encounter a snake or a cat. Park managers have posted signs detailing what you should do if you encounter a mountain lion on the trail.

Other: The route includes trails in both a regional open space preserve and a Santa Clara County park. The melding of the two is seamless on these impeccably maintained trails. You'll find plenty of parking in the several lots along the park access road. Trailhead amenities include restrooms, water, telephones, trashcans, and informational signs. Deer Hollow Farm, a working farm and educational facility available to school and community groups as well as the public, is open from 8:00 a.m. to 4:00 p.m. Tuesday through Sunday. The farm closes at 1:00 p.m. on Wednesday and is closed on Monday.

Finding the trailhead: From Interstate 280 northwest of Cupertino, take the Foothill Expressway exit. Head west on the Foothill Expressway for 0.1 mile to Cristo Rey Drive. Turn right (north) on Cristo Rey Drive and travel 0.6 mile to the roundabout. Take the second roundabout exit, signed for the park. Continue to the park entrance on the left (west). The trailhead is in the lower parking lot adjacent to the restrooms; begin on the paved road behind the gate. *DeLorme Northern California Atlas & Gazetteer:* Page 115 B4. GPS: N37 19.935' W122 05.246.'

The Hike

The history of the Rancho San Antonio park complex encapsulates a story shared by many parks in the San Francisco Bay Area. The Ohlone Indians thrived here for thousands of years before the arrival of Europeans, harvesting oaks for acorns (their staple food) and using other native plants, like the berries of the bay laurel, blackberries, and willow, for food and medicine. They also hunted the woodlands, which then harbored tule elk and bear.

Enter the Spaniards, who set about colonizing California in the late eighteenth century. The Santa Clara mission was established not far south of Rancho San Antonio, and the natives that survived new diseases brought by the intruders were hustled into the mission compound to work and to be "saved."

The park derives its name from its identity during California's long Spanish and Mexican eras. Rancho San Antonio was granted to Juan Prado Mesa who, according to park literature, was a soldier at the San Francisco Presidio and an Indian fighter of some renown. The rancho, like others throughout Alta California, was used to raise cattle for hides and tallow.

After California was incorporated into the United States about the time of the gold rush, part of the rancho was sold to the Snyder family, who maintained a farm, vineyard, and orchard on the land. The county park department and open space district began acquiring the ranch land for a park in 1977.

The route described here links trails in the contiguous county park and open space preserve. The park complex is extremely popular with cyclists, hikers, and trail runners, so be prepared to share the trails with plenty of like-minded visitors. Trail etiquette is important given the high volume of foot and cycling traffic.

Begin by climbing the Hill Trail, where you'll enjoy views east toward the bay. Coyote Trail and the Farm Bypass Trail, which lead west to Wildcat Canyon, are smooth and shady, traversing gently downhill through oak woodlands to the stream corridor. Check out the buckeye trees along the well-graded track, which bear fragrant blooms in spring when they leaf out and heavy fruits in fall that dangle like dingle balls from the bare branches.

Wildcat Creek is the star of the Wildcat Canyon stretch of trail, flowing beneath a dense canopy of bay and oak. A series of bridges span the flow, which is vigorous in winter and slows to a trickle by the end of the dry season.

The return leg swings past Deer Hollow Farm, a working farm and educational center with friendly livestock, old farm equipment including a wagon seeder, an organic garden, and a historic cabin dating back to the days of the Grant Ranch. The loop concludes in the expansive North Meadow, where you'll find a wheelchair-accessible stretch of trail and an enormous heritage bay laurel.

Miles and Directions

0.0 Start by crossing the bridge over Permanente Creek and following the paved road uphill above North Meadow.

0.2 Go left (west) on the Hill Trail (no sign here), climbing up and southwest with views of the bay behind you.

0.4 Pass the junction with the trail to the water tanks on the left (east). Stay right (south) on the Hill Trail.

0.6 Arrive at the four-way junction with the Coyote Trail and the PG&E Trail. Turn right (west) onto the Coyote Trail. You'll cross the unmarked park boundary shortly after you head into the trees.

1.2 Reach the junction with the Farm Bypass Trail. Stay left (west) on the Coyote/Farm Bypass Trail, which continues toward Wildcat Canyon.

1.3 Pass the junction with a trail that drops right (northeast) toward Deer Hollow Farm. Stay left (west) toward the junction with the Wildcat Loop Trail.

1.4 Arrive at the start of the Wildcat Loop Trail, which heads up the lovely, fragrant canyon to the left (west). Cross the first of five bridges as you hike along the stream.

2.0 Cross the last bridge and reach the junction with the Upper Wildcat Canyon Trail. This is the turnaround point; retrace your steps back to the beginning of the Wildcat Loop Trail. (**Options:** The junction of the Wildcat Loop Trail and the Upper Wildcat Canyon Trail is the perfect jumping-off point for those interested in delving farther into Rancho San Antonio's wild lands. Use the trail map to design a loop of your desired length and difficulty.)

2.6 Arrive back at the base of the Wildcat Loop Trail. Stay straight (east) on the trail to Deer Hollow Farm, a broad track that passes through bottomlands along Wildcat Creek.

2.7 Arrive at Deer Hollow Farm and the junction with the Lower Meadow Trail. Proceed through the farm on the roadway/ trail, checking out the garden, livestock, and historic cabin as you go.

2.8 Cross a bridge on the farm's east border and take the log- lined dirt track signed LOWER MEADOW TRAIL (which parallels the paved road). The dirt trail rejoins the roadway 0.1 mile ahead.

3.0 Pass the road to the ranger's office, staying left (east) on the Lower Meadow Trail, then break right (southeast) on the signed pedestrian path that continues toward North Meadow.

3.1 Pass the boundary between the open space preserve and the county park at a large informational kiosk (with maps). Cross the bike path and roadway onto the gravel, wheelchair-accessible Permanente Creek Trail through North Meadow. The heritage bay and an interpretive sign are on the right (west).

3.4 Arrive back at the trailhead parking area, crossing a foot- bridge and passing stretching bars for runners.

8 Stevens Creek/Tony Look and Loop Trails (Stevens Creek County Park)

This broad walk-and-talk trail is perfect for family outings and hikes with friends. Tracing the shoreline of Stevens Creek Reservoir, the route affords views of boaters and the wooded peaks of the Santa Cruz Mountains.

Distance: 2.5 miles out and back (with a little loop)

Approximate hiking time: 1.5 hours

Difficulty: Easy

Trail surface: Dirt roadway, a short loop of singletrack

Best season: Year-round. You may want to avoid the trail for a couple of days after a heavy rain, as it can be muddy.

Other trail users: None (except for a short stretch—less than 0.1 mile—at the junction with the Coyote Ridge Trail)

Canine compatibility: Leashed dogs permitted

Fees and permits: A $6 day-use fee is levied.

Schedule: The park is open from 8:00 a.m. to sunset daily.

Maps: USGS Cupertino; Santa Clara County Park brochure and map to the park available at the trailhead and online

Trail contact: Santa Clara County Parks and Recreation Department, 298 Garden Hill Drive, Los Gatos, CA 95032-7699; (408) 355-2200; www.parkhere.org

Special considerations: The park is home to rattlesnakes and mountain lions. While an encounter is unlikely, caution and common sense are advised. Park managers have posted signs detailing what you should do if you encounter a mountain lion on the trail. Stay on the trail to avoid poison oak. Sudden oak death syndrome, a disease that kills several varieties of native oak woodland species, is found in the park; clean your shoes or boots to avoid transmitting the contagion. Do not remove any soil or vegetation from the area.

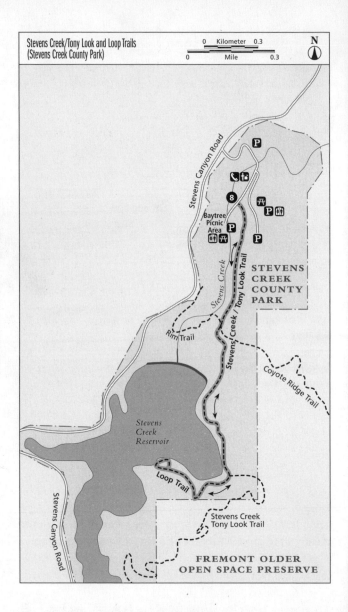

Stevens Creek/Tony Look and Loop Trails
(Stevens Creek County Park)

0   Kilometer   0.3

0   Mile   0.3

N

Stevens Canyon Road

P

8

Baytree
Picnic
Area

P

P

P

STEVENS
CREEK
COUNTY
PARK

Stevens Creek

Stevens Creek / Tony Look Trail

Rim Trail

Coyote Ridge Trail

Stevens
Creek
Reservoir

Loop Trail

Stevens Creek
Tony Look Trail

Stevens Canyon Road

FREMONT OLDER
OPEN SPACE PRESERVE

Other: In the upper lot you'll find the fee station, picnic areas, and plenty of parking. The information station and a phone are about 0.1 mile down the park road. Additional parking, restrooms, and picnic tables are located in the Baytree picnic area just south of the trailhead.

Finding the trailhead: From Interstate 280 in Cupertino, take the Foothill Expressway exit and head west on North Foothill Boulevard. About 0.5 mile from the freeway, North Foothill Boulevard intersects Stevens Creek Boulevard and becomes South Foothill Boulevard; continue west on Foothill. At 0.9 mile South Foothill becomes Stevens Canyon Road. Continue west on Stevens Canyon Road for 1.3 miles to the park entrance on the left (south). Total mileage from the freeway is 2.2 miles. The trailhead is about 0.1 mile down the park access road and 400 feet south of the information station on the left (south) side of the access road. *DeLorme Northern California Atlas & Gazetteer:* Page 115 C4. GPS (upper parking lot): N37 18.404' W122 04.408'. GPS (trailhead): N37 18.252' W122 04.441'.

The Hike

Stevens Creek Reservoir is the primary draw of this county park, and the route described here skirts the shoreline for most of its length. No motorized boats are allowed on the water, so even on the busiest weekends, hikers and other recreationalists aren't bothered by the drone of engines. Instead, a walk along the shoreline treats visitors to vistas of birds and anglers playing on or along the serene lake.

The lakeside trail is broad, allowing families and friends to walk side by side to a little loop overlooking the boat ramp. It is perfect for a weekend outing with the kids, or for an afternoon jog with your best pal (canine or otherwise).

The trail begins alongside Stevens Creek, which flows year-round and supports a nice riparian habitat of cottonwoods, willows, bays, maples, buckeyes, and oaks. The only climb is from the base of the spillway to the top, where the reservoir spreads below the foothills of the Santa Cruz Mountains. In the heat of summer the cool expanse of water is a tease: No swimming is permitted. In winter the surface sparkles under the low-slung sun. The trail hugs the shoreline to a short loop, where side trails offer access to the waterside for fishing and sightseeing, and an old oak offers shade for picnics or naps.

Stevens Creek County Park and its sister, Upper Stevens Creek County Park, are part of a complex of open spaces spanning the ridgetops and valleys of the Santa Cruz Mountains from the Portola Valley south to Los Gatos. They form an undeveloped backdrop to the cities that crowd the South Bay, and a welcome sanctuary for those who crave solitude and natural beauty. But while parks and preserves higher in the mountains boast quiet and seclusion, lower Stevens Creek is a more urban animal. Though enjoyable in many ways, traffic noise from nearby Stevens Canyon Road and the quarry on the north side of the park does intrude.

Miles and Directions

0.0 Start by following the creek south toward the reservoir.

0.5 Reach the junction with the Rim Trail in a shady glade at the base of the spillway. Stay straight (south) on the Tony Look Trail. Just uphill from the junction the Tony Look Trail breaks to the right (north) through a gate, with the Coyote Ridge leading left (south) toward the Fremont Older Open Space Preserve.

0.7 Climb rather steeply to the top of the spillway. Views across the reservoir reach up into the Santa Cruz Mountains.

1.0 Arrive at the junction of the Stevens Creek/Tony Look Trail and the Loop Trail. Go right (south) on the Loop Trail; the Stevens Creek/Tony Look Trail climbs left (east).

1.2 Reach the split in the Loop Trail. You can take the 0.1-mile loop in either direction. Views are of the boat ramp, lake, dam, and the quarry on the north side of Stevens Canyon Road.

1.3 Return to the trail fork and retrace your steps to the trail-head.

2.5 Arrive back at the trailhead.

9 Castle Rock and Castle Rock Falls Tour (Castle Rock State Park)

From weirdly sculpted rock outcrops to a waterfall that plunges more than a hundred feet down a sheer face, this tour will satisfy the thrill-seeker in every hiker.

Distance: 2.6-mile lollipop

Approximate hiking time: 1.5 hours

Difficulty: Moderate due to length and a steady descent and ascent

Trail surface: Dirt singletrack with a short stretch on a wider dirt road

Best season: Year-round

Other trail users: Trail runners, rock climbers

Canine compatibility: Dogs not permitted

Fees and permits: A $6 day-use fee is levied at the trailhead parking lot.

Schedule: The park is open from 6:00 a.m. to sunset daily.

Maps: USGS Castle Rock Ridge; park map and description published online. The Castle Rock Trail Map is available by mail from the Portola and Castle Rock Foundation. Send $2 and a self-addressed stamped envelope to the foundation at 9000 Por-tola State Park Road Box F, La Honda, CA 94020.

Trail contact: California State Parks, Department of Parks and Recreation, 416 Ninth Street, Sacramento, CA 95814; P.O. Box 942896, Sacramento, CA 94296; (800) 777-0369 or (916) 653-6995; www.parks.ca .gov; info@parks.ca.gov. Portola and Castle Rock Foundation, 9000 Portola State Park Road, Box F, La Honda, CA 94020; (650) 948-9098.

Special considerations: The park's faceted and pocked rock formations tempt both experi-enced and inexperienced climb-ers. Please venture onto routes only if you have the training and the proper gear.

Other: Trailhead amenities include plenty of parking, rest-rooms, trashcans, and information boards. Bring your own water.

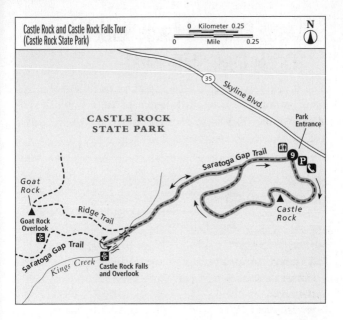

Castle Rock and Castle Rock Falls Tour
(Castle Rock State Park)

0   Kilometer 0.25
0   Mile   0.25

N

CASTLE ROCK
STATE PARK

Skyline Blvd.

Park
Entrance

Saratoga Gap Trail

9   P

Goat
Rock

Ridge Trail

Goat Rock
Overlook

Castle
Rock

Saratoga Gap Trail

Kings Creek

Castle Rock Falls
and Overlook

Finding the trailhead: Castle Rock State Park is at 15000 Skyline Boulevard in Los Gatos. From Interstate 280 in Cupertino, take the Highway 85 exit and head south on Highway 85 to the De Anza Boulevard exit. Go right (south) onto Saratoga Sunnyvale Road, and continue for 2.4 miles to Highway 9/Big Basin Way. Go right (west) on Highway 9 for 7.3 miles to Skyline Boulevard. Turn left (south) on Skyline Boulevard (Highway 35) and travel 2.6 miles to the park entrance on the right (west).

Alternatively, from Highway 17 in Los Gatos, take the Bear Creek Road exit. Follow Bear Creek Road east for 0.3 mile to Black Road. Turn left on Black Road and travel for 4.4 scenic, winding miles to Skyline Boulevard. Turn right (north) on Skyline Boulevard and go 3.7 miles to the park entrance, which is on the left (west). The trailhead is at the west boundary of the lot. *DeLorme Northern California Atlas and Gazetteer:* Page 115 B5. GPS: N37 13.825' W122 05.762.'

The Hike

What a trip! From the pocked, overhanging faces of Castle Rock to the observation deck jutting out over the 80-foot falls at the headwaters of Kings Creek, the scenic destinations on this tour are enchanting.

Castle Rock, the park's high point, is more a palace for forest gnomes than princesses. Perched on the crest of the Santa Cruz Mountains, its sandstone faces host a honeycomb of holds, shallow caves, and, on dry sunny days, crowds of climbers. Views are obscured by the dense forest that surrounds the rock and its smaller counterparts, but you can pull up a piece of the stone apron that surrounds the base and enjoy the athletic showmanship.

The views are downstream, seen from the deck that overlooks Castle Rock Falls. Climbing routes lie on either side of the cascade, which stains a long slab diving into the San Lorenzo Creek watershed. The steep, thickly forested ridges of the Santa Cruz range fold westward to the horizon, with exposed rock outcrops jutting from the canopy on the nearest slope to the north.

The trails linking the rock and the falls cruise through a dense woodland of pines and oaks, with very little sunlight filtering through. Mosses cling to the boulders lining the trails—at least to those faces that aren't used by climbers—and deadfall jams the creek down to the falls. On a foggy day the atmosphere is primordial, with the slightest wind shifting the boughs overhead and rocks looming out of the woods suddenly, like giant trolls.

The elevation change from the trek's high point at Castle Rock to its low point at Castle Rock Falls feels significant but is not particularly strenuous. Slopes are moderate, and easily tackled by hikers who watch their pace.

Miles and Directions

0.0   Start by heading left (south) and uphill on the trail to Castle Rock. A trail sign about 50 yards farther directs you right and up on the forested singletrack.

0.2   At the trail junction above the Isabella Soria and Nina Bingham Memorial Trees go right (north) on the trail (now a dirt road covered in leaf litter). Rock formations dot the forest floor to the left (southwest).

0.3   Arrive at Castle Rock, which rises north of a large clearing. An outhouse is to the right (east). A trail marker points the way north to Saratoga Gap Trail. The singletrack curls down and around the base of the rock, passing caves where climbers can hang like bats while they contemplate their next moves.

0.5   At the trail sign switchback right and downhill toward the Saratoga Gap Trail.

0.8   Trail signs keep you on track as climbers' trails branch off the main route.

1.0   Cross a series of little wooden bridges to the trail intersection with the Saratoga Gap Trail. Go left (west) on the Saratoga Gap Trail toward Castle Rock Falls. The trail follows a log-cluttered seasonal stream down to Kings Creek.

1.5   Cross a bridge to the junction of the Saratoga Gap and Ridge Trails. Go left (west) on the Saratoga Gap Trail to Castle Rock Falls.

1.7   Arrive at the overlook of the falls. After checking out the cascade and the views, retrace your steps to the junction of the Saratoga Gap Trail and the Castle Rock Trail.

2.4   Reach the junction of the Saratoga Gap and Castle Rock Trails. Stay right (east) on the Saratoga Gap Trail, which ascends past a cavernous rock toward the parking lot. Ignore the climbers' trail that leads to the rock.

2.6   Arrive back at the trailhead and parking area.

10 Circle Corral and Bass Lake Loop (Joseph D. Grant County Park)

Open meadows, meandering creeks, a historic corral, and a small lake lie along this loop through cattle country in the scenic Halls Valley.

Distance: 4.5-mile loop

Approximate hiking time: 2.5 hours

Difficulty: More challenging due to length and several ascents

Trail surface: Ranch road and dirt singletrack

Best season: Spring and fall. The trail can be hiked year-round, but there's little shade so it may be hot in summer and trails may get sloppy during and after winter rains.

Other trail users: Equestrians, trail runners

Canine compatibility: Leashed dogs permitted in some areas of the park

Fees and permits: A $6 fee is charged for entry to the developed areas around the park headquarters and campgrounds. No fee is charged to park at the Grant Lake trailhead, where this loop begins.

Schedule: The park is open from 8:00 a.m. to sunset daily. The trail can be hiked from sunrise to sunset, but you must park your vehicle legally outside the park boundary.

Maps: USGS Lick Observatory; Santa Clara County Park brochure and map available at the trailhead and online

Trail contact: Santa Clara County Parks and Recreation Department, 298 Garden Hill Drive, Los Gatos, CA 95032-7699; (408) 355-2200; www .parkhere.org

Special considerations: The park is home to rattlesnakes and mountain lions. While an encounter is unlikely, caution and common sense are advised. Information signs posted at the trailhead provide information on how to react if you should meet a mountain lion.

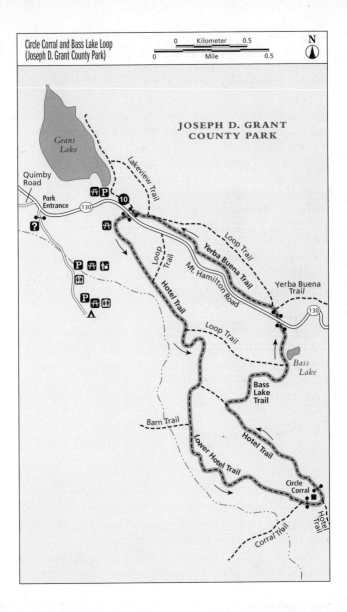

Circle Corral and Bass Lake Loop
(Joseph D. Grant County Park)

Kilometer
0   0.5
Mile
0   0.5

N

JOSEPH D. GRANT
COUNTY PARK

Grant
Lake

Quimby
Road

Park
Entrance

130

10

Lakeview Trail

Loop Trail

Yerba Buena Trail

Mt. Hamilton Road

Yerba Buena
Trail

130

Loop Trail

Loop Trail

Bass
Lake

Hotel Trail

Bass Lake
Trail

Barn Trail

Hotel Trail

Lower Hotel Trail

Circle
Corral

Hotel
Trail

Corral Trail

Other: Water, a restroom, and information are available at the trailhead. Trails are subject to temporary closure to cyclists and equestrians; contact the park at (408) 355-2200 option 7 for current trail conditions.

Finding the trailhead: From U.S. Highway 101 or Interstate 680, take the Alum Rock Road exit. Follow Alum Rock Road east to Mt. Hamilton Road and turn right (south). The park entrance is about 8 miles from the junction of Alum Rock and Mount Hamilton Roads; the trailhead parking area is just beyond the main entrance on the left (north) side. Alternatively, you can take the Capital Expressway exit from US 101 and follow it east for 1.4 miles to Quimby Road. Turn right (east) and take Quimby Road for 6.8 miles (the last 4 miles are narrow and winding) to Mount Hamilton Road. Turn right (south) on Mount Hamilton Road for 0.2 mile to the trailhead parking area. *DeLorme Northern California Atlas & Gazetteer:* Page 116 1B. GPS: N37 20.586' W121 42.975'.

The Hike

The Halls Valley looks a lot like neighboring Santa Clara Valley did before the dawn of the silicon age. Not as untouched as when the Ohlone Indians worked the woodlands, harvesting oaks for acorns and hunting for game, but the legacy of its days as a rancho lingers.

Tangible evidence of the park's agricultural heritage include the ranch roads upon which many of the trails lie, the cattle that continue to graze in some areas as part of a resource management program, and the Circle Corral, its fence boards silvered by the sun and stained green and white with lichen. The old ranch house sits on a rise on the valley floor overlooking San Felipe Creek.

Less tangible are the ghosts of the families who worked the land, and later sought its preservation. There was the original rancho grantee, Jose de Jesus Bernal, and Kentucky native Samuel Boughton; other owners were members of the infamous Donner Party, according to park literature. But perhaps most significant was the park's namesake Joseph Grant, who used part of a fortune earned running the family dry goods store to acquire the property. Guests at the ranch included President Herbert Hoover. Grant's daughter, Josephine, who lived on the ranch until she died in the early 1970s, donated the land to a preservation organization; it was later purchased by Santa Clara County as a park.

The route begins by following San Felipe Creek downstream through grassy bottomlands rich with wildflowers in spring. Cows, barbed-wire fences, and old oaks edge the route. Red-tailed hawks wheel and screech overhead, while daring ground squirrels dash across the open road and dive into burrows to avoid becoming dinner. The creek is a distant partner to the right (east), its passage marked by a line of verdant riparian habitat.

The loop curls through the Circle Corral at its southern end, then begins a long but not terribly difficult climb toward the junction with the singletrack path to Bass Lake. More climbing through sunny meadows leads to the small, reed-rimmed pond, where you can pull up a seat on the picnic bench and rest before tackling the rolling downhill run on the Yerba Buena Trail back to the trailhead.

Miles and Directions

0.0 Start by following the Yerba Buena Trail up and right (south) from the trailhead.

0.1 At the junction with the Loop Trail turn right (west), pass through a gate, then cross Mount Hamilton Road. Beyond a second gate you'll reach the junction with the Hotel Trail.

Turn right (west), heading downhill on the broad Hotel Trail.

0.5 Reach a second junction of the Hotel and Loop Trails; stay straight (south and downhill) on the Hotel Trail. About 75 yards beyond you'll pass the access trail to park facilities, including the visitor center and the ranch house. Again, stay straight (south) on the Hotel Trail.

0.8 Pass another intersection with the Loop Trail, again staying straight (south) on the Hotel Trail.

1.2 At the intersection of the Hotel Loop with the Lower Hotel Loop, stay straight (right/south) on the Lower Hotel Loop. The Hotel Loop climbs to the left (southeast) to the junction with the Bass Lake Trail, a nice option if you want to shorten the loop.

1.4 Pass the junction with the Barn Trail. Stay left (south) on the Lower Hotel Trail. The trail parallels the creek and its riparian zone.

2.0 Pass through a gate.

2.2 The Corral Trail intersects the Lower Hotel Trail. Go left (east) on the Corral Trail and pass through the enclosures of the picturesque Circle Corral. Make a hard left on the Hotel Trail, passing through a gate, and begin a rolling climb on a red-earth ranch road.

2.8 Arrive at the Bass Lake Trail junction. Views north down the Halls Valley are lovely. Go right (east and uphill) on the Bass Lake Trail.

3.1 Pass a pond that dries up in late summer and fall.

3.2 Circle out of the hollow that holds the pond and into the hollow that holds Bass Lake. A narrow singletrack trail crosses the dam on the west side of the lake, then climbs the steep hillside toward Mount Hamilton Road above.

3.5 At the roadside, pass through a gate via a short ladder, cross Mount Hamilton Road, and pass through another gate to the junction of the Loop Trail and the Yerba Buena Trail. Turn left (north) on the Yerba Buena Trail. The singletrack is

off-limits to cyclists, but tire tracks in the dirt indicate the
route is poached.

3.8 Pass the cut-off trail on the right (east), continuing straight
(north) on the Yerba Buena Trail.

4.1 The route rolls over hills adjacent to Mount Hamilton Road,
passing through a gate.

4.3 Pass yet another junction with the Loop Trail, staying straight
(northwest) on the Yerba Buena Trail.

4.4 Arrive back at the first junction of the Loop Trail. Continue
straight (northwest) on the Yerba Buena Trail, retracing your
steps.

4.5 Arrive at the parking area and trailhead.

11 Coyote Creek Parkway and Hellyer County Park

A walk–and–talk trail, a workout trail, and a meander through riparian habitat, this popular paved route anchors a narrow greenbelt along pretty Coyote Creek.

Distance: 4.6 miles out and back

Approximate hiking time: 3 hours

Difficulty: Moderate due only to trail length

Trail surface: Paved

Best season: Year-round. Portions of the trail may be closed in winter due to flooding; call the trail hotline at (408) 355-2200 option 7 for current conditions.

Other trail users: Cyclists (including bike commuters), trail runners

Canine compatibility: Leashed dogs permitted

Fees and permits: A $6 per vehicle day-use fee is levied at the Hellyer County Park trailhead.

Schedule: Hellyer County Park is open from 8:00 a.m. to sunset daily.

Maps: USGS San Jose East; Santa Clara County Park brochure and map to Hellyer County Park available at the trailhead and online

Trail contact: Santa Clara County Parks and Recreation Department, 298 Garden Hill Drive, Los Gatos, CA 95032-7699; (408) 355-2200; www.parkhere.org

Special considerations: This trail is very popular and can be crowded with both cyclists and hikers. Most cyclists are courteous and observe speed limits, but some don't, so be wary.

Other: Trailhead amenities include restrooms and picnic areas. A dog park and velodrome are about 0.1 mile north along the Hellyer County Park road. Cottonwood Lake is stocked with rainbow trout in winter and spring. Bring drinking water.

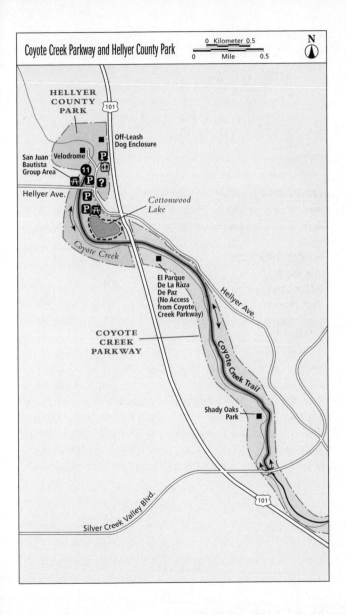

Coyote Creek Parkway and Hellyer County Park

0 Kilometer 0.5
0 Mile 0.5

N

HELLYER COUNTY PARK

101

Off-Leash Dog Enclosure

San Juan Bautista Group Area

Velodrome

11

Hellyer Ave.

Cottonwood Lake

Coyote Creek

El Parque De La Raza De Paz (No Access from Coyote Creek Parkway)

Hellyer Ave.

COYOTE CREEK PARKWAY

Coyote Creek Trail

Shady Oaks Park

101

Silver Creek Valley Blvd.

Finding the trailhead: From U.S. Highway 101 in San Jose, head south to the Hellyer Avenue exit. Go west on Hellyer Avenue to the stop sign. Turn right (north) and go 0.2 mile to the park entrance. Park in the first lot to your left (west) at the San Juan Bautista picnic area. The paved path is on the west side of the picnic grounds. *DeLorme Northern California Atlas & Gazetteer:* Page 115 B6, B7. GPS: N37 17.117' W121 48.762'.

The Hike

The Coyote Creek Parkway stretches more than 15 miles from Hellyer County Park in south San Jose to Anderson Lake County Park in Morgan Hill. This linear park is a Santa Clara County treasure, tracing Coyote Creek on its northward run to San Francisco Bay and protecting the fragile riparian habitat that lines its banks. It links open spaces, neighborhoods, business parks, and schools, offering an alternative, human-powered route for commuters and visitors alike.

The recreational opportunities on the paved trail are many: hiking, running, bike riding, bird watching, and just sitting alongside the creek and relaxing. On any day of the week you'll encounter extended families cycling from park to park, couples of all ages walking hand in hand, runners decked out in everything from form-fitting Lycra to blue jeans, and kids risking a nasty case of poison oak by slipping down to creekside pools to fish or skip stones.

Though adjacent urban development, from the business parks and neighborhoods mentioned above to intersections with major roadways and interstate overpasses, precludes this as a wildland getaway, the trail offers a quick escape for hikers. The stretch described here skirts pretty Cottonwood Lake, passes under noisy US 101, then rambles into quieter territory where civilization is filtered by the thick growth of willow, bay, and sycamore along the creek banks. Views open onto the hills that form the eastern rampart of the Santa Clara Valley. Shady Oak Park, with its tot lot, picnic tables, and playing green, is the turnaround point for the easy trek.

The park's location at the edge of dense urban development, and Coyote Creek's importance as a natural resource—it's fed by one of the largest watersheds in the Santa Clara Valley, with its headwaters in the Diablo Range—prompted its preservation. The concept germinated in the 1960s, was backed by a number of public entities including the city of San Jose, Santa Clara County, and the Coastal Conservancy, and has been the subject of ongoing implementation and improvement from then on.

You can hop on the parkway (part of the Bay Area Ridge Trail) anywhere along its length. At Anderson Lake County Park, outside Morgan Hill at the trail's southern endpoint, a dirt equestrian track runs parallel to the parkway. The path also links to the Coyote Ranch historic site and the Coyote Creek Golf Course.

Options: As mentioned above, you can continue south on the parkway for miles. You'll find trailheads at Blossom Hill Road, Bernal Road, Metcalf Road, Burnett Avenue, and Cochrane Road, as well as access to a number of parks and rest areas that present other turnaround or point-to-point (car shuttle) options.

San Jose offers more than 50 miles of paved urban trails that are showcased at www.sjparks.org/trails. Of particular interest are the Los Gatos Creek Trail, which links the Lexington Dam, Los Gatos, Campbell, and San Jose, and the Guadalupe River Trail, which features flood-control elements that have been creatively integrated into the greenbelt, artwork, access to a historic neighborhood, and views of the city's skyline. More information on the Los Gatos Creek Trail is at www.sjparks.org/Trails/LosGatos/LosGatos.asp. For more on the Guadalupe River Trail, visit www.sjparks.org/Trails/GRiver/index.asp.

Miles and Directions

0.0 Start on the paved path to the west of the picnic grounds.

0.1 Pass under Hellyer Avenue, then head up and past a bridge that links to the roadway. Stay straight (south) on the paved path, which is bordered on the left (east) by the parking area for Cottonwood Lake and on the right (west) by the full but placid creek.

0.4 Emerge from the riparian zone at a trail intersection with the path around Cottonwood Lake. Continue south on the Coyote Creek Parkway, which skirts the lawn encircling the lake. Highway noise is a constant companion for the next half mile or so.

0.7 The paved trail that circles the lake joins the parkway from the left (north). Continue south, passing under the freeway. You can find a hint of nature here, as doves roost in the girders supporting the roadbed.

1.2 The highway noise has faded and the creek bottom has opened up, offering views up and left (east) onto grassy hillsides.

1.5 Pass a mile marker.

1.6 The path hopscotches through pockets of urban development and natural habitat, with views opening again onto the grass-covered hills and the unyielding glass and concrete walls of office buildings.

1.8 Meet an access trail that leads left (east) into trailside developments. Beyond, the path climbs over a rise, then is wedged between the creek and a business park.

2.3 Arrive at the pretty bridge that spans the creek and leads west into Shady Oaks Park. This is the turnaround point; retrace your steps to the trailhead.

4.6 Arrive back at the trailhead and parking area.

12 English Camp Loop (Almaden Quicksilver County Park)

The remnants of a historic mining camp, where the families of men excavating valuable ores from the steep hills once abided, is at the apex of this loop.

Distance: 3.5-mile loop

Approximate hiking time: 2 hours

Difficulty: Moderate due to length and steady climbing and descents

Trail surface: Dirt mining roads, singletrack on a portion of the Deep Gulch Trail

Best season: Spring and fall, though the trail is passable year-round.

Other trail users: Mountain bikers, equestrians, trail runners

Canine compatibility: Leashed dogs permitted

Fees and permits: None

Schedule: The park is open from sunrise to sunset daily.

Maps: USGS Santa Teresa Hills; Santa Clara County Park brochure and map to the park available at the trailhead and online

Trail contact: Santa Clara County Parks and Recreation Department, 298 Garden Hill Drive, Los Gatos, CA 95032-7699; (408) 355-2200; www.parkhere.org

Special considerations: This is mountain lion and rattlesnake country. An encounter is unlikely, but use caution and common sense when hiking in the park.

Other: Use caution when exploring the historic mining sites, obey caution signs, and stay on the trails (this will also protect you from contact with poison oak). Leave all artifacts on site for the next visitor to enjoy. Trailhead facilities include plenty of parking, picnic sites, trashcans, and restrooms. Bring drinking water. Park trails are subject to temporary closure to mountain bikers and equestrians in winter; contact the trails hotline at (408) 355-2200 option 7 for current conditions.

English Camp Loop (Almaden Quicksilver County Park)

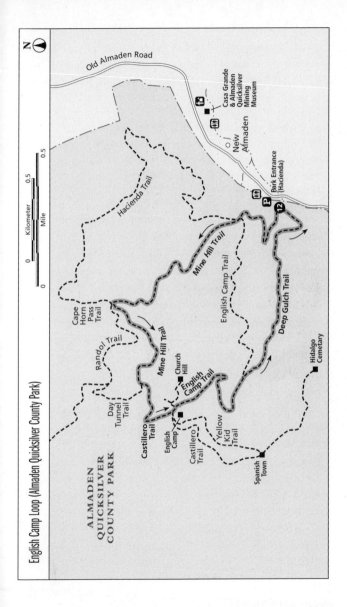

Finding the trailhead: To reach the Hacienda trailhead from Interstate 280 in San Jose, take Highway 17 south toward Los Gatos to Highway 85. Exit onto Highway 85 southbound and continue to the Almaden Expressway exit. Head southeast on Almaden Expressway for 4.2 miles to Old Almaden Road. Turn right (south) on Old Almaden Road and travel 4.2 miles, through the charming village of New Almaden, to the park entrance on the right (west). The Hacienda trailhead is adjacent to the information board on the west side of the parking area. *DeLorme Northern California Atlas & Gazetteer:* Page 115 B6. GPS: N37 10.449' W121 49.510'.

The Hike

Mercury, called quicksilver, drew miners from around the world to the New Almaden Quicksilver Mine. For more than 135 years, from the time of Mexican rule in California to 1976, the rock containing quicksilver, called cinnabar, was extracted from these hills. Used to process gold and silver ore, the mine produced more than eighty three million pounds of mercury during its long history, according to park literature.

The loop to English Camp, one of several camps established in the hills during the mine's long life, follows wide gently graded mining roads through scenic landscapes with great views. For the first mile or so you look out across the steep New Almaden Canyon, which opens eastward on the southern Santa Clara Valley. At the Cape Horn Pass intersection, views extend north to the San Jose cityscape and the blue bay beyond. The hills are covered in oak woodland, with patches of chaparral on the sunny south-facing slopes, and most of the trails are wide enough for hikers to walk side by side and comfortably pass other trail users.

But it's the history that enlivens the loop, from the decrepit cabin settling into the hillside below the camp to the rusting remnants of equipment from the Hacienda reduction works, protected behind a chain-link fence at trail's end.

Periwinkle, a staple of English gardens, grows in patches as you near the camp, which occupies a saddle at more than 1,300 feet overlooking the Almaden Valley. There's a lot to explore here—collapsed and decaying buildings, monuments, a church on a hill. Interpretive signs describe life in the camp, from the families who traveled from Cornwall, England, so their men could work the mine to the camp school, with a picture showing the class of 1886. Picnic tables in the shade are perfect for lunch or a snack.

The last section of trail follows Deep Gulch down to the valley floor. No sign of mining here—after you pass the tailings pile (mounded rubble left over from the extraction process), the path narrows to singletrack and drops through thick forest to the valley floor. The rusted remnants of the Hacienda reduction works recline in what now is a meadow. Mine reclamation at its best!

Miles and Directions

0.0 Start by heading uphill on the Mine Hill Trail, which is also part of the Almaden Quicksilver Historic Trail. You'll pass occasional interpretive markers along the route.

0.4 Climb to a four-way trail intersection with the English Camp Trail (on the left/south) and the Hacienda Trail (on the right/north). Stay straight on the Mine Hill Trail.

1.2 Arrive at the trail intersection below Cape Horn Pass. Go left (up and west) on the Mine Hill Trail (now also part of the Bay Area Ridge Trail and the Anza Historical Trail). The Randol and Cape Horn Pass Trails are to the right (north) of the Mine Hill Trail.

1.7 Pass the Day Tunnel Trail on the right (north). Stay left (west) on the wide Mine Hill Trail. Watch the left side of the track for an interesting bay tree; its gnarly roots jut from the hillside in a Gothic tangle, the perfect gnome home.

1.9 Reach the junction of the Mine Hill Trail and the Castillero Trail. Bigleaf maples line this ascending stretch.

2.2 Arrive at English Camp. The English Camp, Church Hill, and Castillero Trails meet here, with the Yellow Kid Trail marker visible just uphill from the camp's monument. Explore the camp, then head left (south and downhill) past the picnic tables on the English Camp Trail.

`2.5 At the junction of the English Camp Trail and the Deep Gulch Trail turn right (west) on the Deep Gulch Trail. Pass the tailings pile, an interpretive marker, and through a clearing before the trail narrows to singletrack and begins to drop along Deep Gulch, heading east. The stream itself is below to the left (north); the track traverses the hillside above through a colorful forest thick with poison oak.

3.4 Meet a fence line at the bottom of the descent, pass through a gate, and cross the cobbled stream into the meadow. Go left (northeast) on the singletrack toward the rusting mine machinery and the trailhead.

3.5 Arrive back at the parking lot.

13 Coyote Peak/Ridge Trail Loop (Santa Teresa County Park)

Even on sunny weekend afternoons the trails at Santa Teresa County Park remain uncrowded—a pleasant surprise given the stunning vistas of the Santa Clara Valley.

Distance: 1.7-mile lollipop

Approximate hiking time: 1.5 hours

Difficulty: More challenging due to steep pitches both uphill and down

Trail surface: Dirt ranch roads

Best season: Spring and fall, though the trail can be hiked year-round. Trails may be muddy for a couple of days after a heavy winter rain.

Other trail users: Mountain bikers, equestrians, trail runners

Canine compatibility: Leashed dogs permitted

Fees and permits: A $6 day-use fee is levied. The automated fee station is in the first parking lot.

Schedule: The park is open daily from 8:00 a.m. to sunset.

Maps: USGS Santa Teresa Hills; Santa Clara County Park brochure and map to the park available at the trailhead and online

Trail contact: Santa Clara County Parks and Recreation Department, 298 Garden Hill Drive, Los Gatos, CA 95032-7699; (408) 355-2200; www .parkhere.org

Special considerations: This is mountain lion and rattle-snake country. An encounter is unlikely, and park managers have installed information signs on how to behave if you meet a mountain lion. Remain on trails to avoid damaging critical habitat.

Other: The park is very popular with mountain bikers. While proper trail etiquette requires cyclists to yield to hikers, the trails are wide enough for both users to pass easily. Trailhead amenities include picnic tables and restrooms. Additional picnic facilities and potable water (along with a volleyball court and

Coyote Peak/Ridge Trail Loop (Santa Teresa County Park)

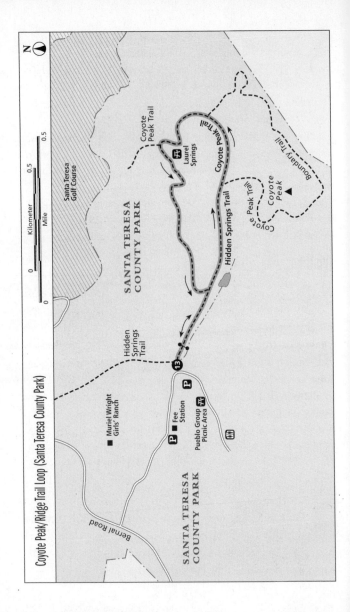

horseshoe pits) are at the Pueblo group picnic area at the end of the park road. The picnic area is available by reservation only. Trails are subject to temporary closure to mountain bikers and equestrians in winter. Call the trails hotline at (408) 335-2200 option 7 for current conditions.

Finding the trailhead: From U.S. Highway 101 in San Jose, head south to the Bernal Road exit. Go west on Bernal Road for 2.8 miles to the park entrance on the left (east). Proceed up the park road 0.5 mile, past the fee station, to the first large parking lot on the right (west). The trailhead is across the park road at the gate and information board. *DeLorme Northern California Atlas & Gazetteer:* Page 115 B7. GPS: N37 12.840' W121 47.133'.

The Hike

Perched on the urban interface, a hike in Santa Teresa County Park is by no means a backcountry experience. But it's also by no means unworthy of a hiker's attention. With views that rival the best in the area, easy access, moderately challenging trails, and dollops of wilderness dropped here and there along the loop, you won't regret time spent here.

The park has a history almost as convoluted as the suburban landscape it rises above. The park brochure lays this out in great detail, from the Ohlone Indians who lived in villages in the Santa Teresa Hills for thousands of years to the acquisition of parcels by Silicon Valley icon IBM. Once part of a rancho settled by Jose Joaquin Bernal, a member of Juan Bautista de Anza's 1776 pioneering expedition into Alta California, over the years these acres have passed through many hands, been grazed by Spanish cattle, planted in orchards, mined for quicksilver, used by a fertilizer company, and developed for recreation.

The county began acquiring land for the park back in the 1950s, with the first parcels developed as the Santa Teresa Golf Course, in the forefront of views from the Ridge Trail. The latest acquisitions occurred in the 1990s, giving the park a total of 1,688 acres.

Coyote Peak is the high point, at more than 1,100 feet, and topped with radio towers. This loop traverses the grasslands and hollows below the summit, climbing first through wildflower fields and pockets of oaks along the Hidden Springs drainage, which holds water year-round. A saddle below the peak affords great views east of the Diablo Range and Mount Hamilton, north across the sometimes smoggy city of San Jose, and west to the ridges of the Santa Cruz Mountains and Mount Umunhum with its concrete box topper (a remnant of an Air Force installation) on the summit.

Traversing on the Ridge Trail, you'll pass through alternating oak woodland and grassland, with the shade and rock outcrops of Laurel Spring offering the chance for a breather after a relatively steep descent and before a relatively steep climb back to the trailhead. Set a comfortable pace, and all the climbs and descents along this route are well within the ability of most hikers.

Miles and Directions

0.0 Start beyond the gate on the signed Hidden Springs Trail, the second trail to the right. The route climbs on a wide ranch road.

0.1 Pass a gate and enter the Hidden Springs drainage.

0.2 At the junction with the Ridge Trail (the return route) stay right (east) on the Hidden Springs Trail.

0.3 Pass a small pond (dry in late summer and fall) on the right (south) and keep climbing.

0.5 The Hidden Springs Trail dead-ends at the junction with the Coyote Peak Trail. Coyote Peak is up and to the right (south), unmistakable with its crown of towers. Turn left (east and downhill) on the Coyote Peak Trail, enjoying the views as you drop under the power line toward the valley floor. The golf course and surrounding backyards are laid out at your feet.

0.7 At the junction of the Coyote Peak and Boundary Trails, stay left (north and downhill) on the Coyote Peak Trail. A huge outcrop containing greenish serpentine, California's state rock, rises alongside the trail, and you can occasionally hear the smack of a club against a golf ball below.

0.9 Curl down to the Ridge Trail junction and turn left (west) into Laurel Spring, where you'll find a picnic table sheltered by . . . yup, laurels. Beyond the shady dell, its boundary marked by large rock outcrops, the Ridge Trail begins to ascend, sometimes steeply, toward the trailhead.

1.4 Finish the climb after a roller-coaster traverse of the north-facing slopes overlooking San Jose and Santa Clara. As you curve west toward the trailhead, you'll have views of Mount Umunhum.

1.5 Reach the junction of the Ridge Trail and the Hidden Springs Trail. Turn right and retrace your steps from here to the trail-head.

1.7 Arrive back at the parking area.

14 Los Cerritos Trail (Calero Reservoir County Park)

Well-groomed ranch roads lead up onto a ridge where views spread north across blue Calero Reservoir, east into the Diablo Range, and south down the scenic Santa Clara Valley.

Distance: 3.3-mile loop
Approximate hiking time: 2 hours
Difficulty: More challenging due to length and some steep climbs and descents
Trail surface: Dirt ranch roads
Best season: Spring for the wildflower displays, but the trail is pleasant year-round. Allow trails to dry out for a couple of days after a heavy winter rain to avoid mud.
Other trail users: Equestrians, trail runners
Canine compatibility: Dogs not permitted except in the picnic area
Fees and permits: None
Schedule: The park is open from 8:00 a.m. to sunset daily.
Maps: USGS Santa Teresa Hills; Santa Clara County Park brochure and map available at the trailhead and online

Trail contact: Santa Clara County Parks and Recreation Department, 298 Garden Hill Drive, Los Gatos, CA 95032-7699; (408) 355-2200; www.parkhere.org
Special considerations: This is mountain lion and rattlesnake country. An encounter is unlikely, but use caution and common sense when hiking in the park. Park managers have posted signs describing recommended behavior should you meet a mountain lion on the route. Encountering horses and their riders, on the other hand, is very likely. While trail etiquette calls for equestrians to yield to hikers, it's often easier for hikers to step aside to make way for horses. These trails are wide enough that all users can share easily.
Other: Trailhead amenities include picnic tables, restrooms,

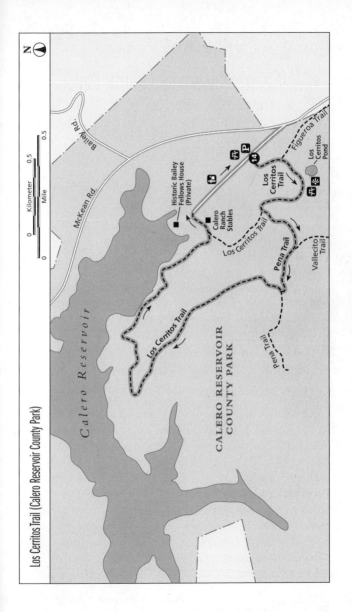

Los Cerritos Trail (Calero Reservoir County Park)

and an information kiosk. Bring drinking water. The park's visitor center is at the north end of the parking area. Calero Ranch Stables is another half mile down the park road, near the historic (private) Bailey Fellows House. For information about boarding, horse rentals, and trail rides call (408) 268-2567. Trails are subject to temporary closure to mountain bikers and equestrians in winter. Call the trails hotline at (408) 335-2200 option 7 for current conditions.

Finding the trailhead: From U.S. Highway 101 south of San Jose take the Bailey Avenue exit. Go southwest on Bailey Avenue for 3.2 miles to McKean Road. Turn left (south) on McKean Road for 0.6 mile to the park entrance on the right (west). The trailhead parking area is 0.1 mile down the park road on the right (east), and the trailhead is across the road at the information board. *DeLorme Northern California Atlas & Gazetteer:* Page 115 C7. GPS: N37 10.481' W121 45.668'.

The Hike

South of San Jose the landscape is dominated by rolling hills with open faces blanketed in grasses and wildflowers, and folds shaded by oaks, bays, and buckeyes. Classic northern California, this is the setting for Calero Reservoir and the parklands that surround it.

This loop takes you into Calero's backcountry, up past scenic Los Cerritos Pond and through shady oak woodlands onto a ridge from which views spread north across Calero Reservoir to San Jose, east into the Diablo Range, and south down the Santa Clara Valley. The park is known for its wildflower displays in spring and summer but offers pleasant walking year-round.

The trail winds for a mile or so along the shores of the reservoir. Built in the 1930s, the lake attracts boaters and licensed anglers, who are advised to release the bass they catch here, as the water is contaminated with mercury from nearby quicksilver mines. Tempting as the water looks on hot summer afternoons after a long hike, swimming is prohibited. Migratory birds winter on the lakeshore, sharing the airspace with resident raptors, songbirds, and shorebirds, a lure for birders.

On the south lakeshore you'll find the Bailey Fellows House, an architecturally compelling historic home that is privately owned and off-limits to park visitors. It was built in the late 1860s by rancher Boargenes Bailey, who married a member of the hard-pressed 1848 Lassen Party, which took the "long way" to California. Bailey raised his family on the property, where he also ran cattle, planted an orchard, and maintained a farm. Later, in the 1930s, lawyer and judge Edward Fellows and his wife acquired the house and property. The judge was killed in an accident in the mid-1960s, and the property subsequently passed into public ownership.

The historic home is surrounded by Calero Ranch Stables, which boards and pastures horses. The trails are plenty wide enough to share with riders. Pass carefully and respectfully through the stables on your way back to the trailhead; please don't feed the horses.

Miles and Directions

0.0 Start by heading southwest up the signed Access Trail.

0.2 At the junction with the Los Cerritos Trail, go right (west) and uphill.

0.3 Reach Los Cerritos Pond, where you'll find an interpretive sign, a hitching post, and an observation deck shaded by an oak. Proceed uphill from the pond, enjoying the views that open east over the stables and reservoir.

0.6 Turn left (west) on the Pena Trail; the Los Cerritos Trail is an option for the return route.

0.8 A steady climb through scattered oaks and wild oats leads to the Vallecito Trail. Stay right (and up) on the Pena Trail, enjoying views down into the little wooded valley on the left (south) and the much bigger, Santa Clara Valley on the right (northeast).

1.0 Top out at the junction of the Pena and Los Cerritos Trails on the ridge crest. The views here are stunning in all directions. When you've had your fill, go right (east and downhill) on the Los Cerritos Trail.

1.3 Pass through a gate as you roller-coaster north down the ridge toward the reservoir, with views of Mount Umunhum (with a distinctive concrete "box" on the summit) and San Jose ahead.

1.8 The trail curls southward, away from the reservoir.

2.0 Sweep down through grasses to the shoreline, where birds hang out when boats aren't disturbing them.

2.8 Pass through two gates and along a fenced pasture to the junction with the access trail to the stables. You can either follow the access trail through the stables to the park road and return to the trailhead that way, or continue on the Los Cerritos Trail. To take the stable route go left (east) and pass through the paddocks to the park road. (**Option:** From the junction with the trail to the stables, you can return via the Los Cerritos, Pena, and Access Trails. Go right (south) on Los Cerritos Trail for 0.3 mile to the Pena Trail junction, then turn left (east and downhill), and continue past Los Cerritos Pond to the Access Trail and the trailhead. This option brings the total to 3.7 miles.)

2.9 Reach the paved park road and turn right (south).

3.3 Arrive back at the trailhead and parking area.

15 Top of the Ridge Tour (Henry Coe State Park)

From the top of the ridge, it's all about the views. On a clear day the Monument and Ponderosa Trails open on a world that extends from Monterey Bay to the Sierra Nevada. Hitch the vistas to the solitude, and you're about as close to paradise as you'll come on a trail.

Distance: 2.3 miles of interlocking lollipop loops

Approximate hiking time: 1.5 hours

Difficulty: Moderate due to elevation gain and loss on the Monument Trail

Trail surface: Dirt singletrack, dirt road, a short section of pavement

Best season: Spring (when the wildflowers bloom) and fall (when the weather is good)

Other trail users: Mountain bikers and equestrians on Hobbs Road and Manzanita Point Road. The trails themselves are reserved for hikers only.

Canine compatibility: No dogs permitted on the trails for this tour. Leashed dogs are permitted in paved areas of the park and on the Live Oak Trail.

Fees and permits: A $5 day-use fee is levied.

Schedule: The park is open from 8:00 a.m. to sunset daily.

Maps: USGS Mount Sizer; park maps available at the trailhead visitor center

Trail contact: Henry W. Coe State Park, 9000 East Dunne Avenue, Morgan Hill, CA 95037; (408) 779-2728; www.parks.ca.gov. The Pine Ridge Association maintains a park Web site at www.coepark.org.

Special considerations: Henry Coe is about as wild as it gets. The park's inhabitants include coyotes, raccoons, wild pigs, mountain lions, and rattlesnakes. None pose a serious threat to hikers, but you are advised to use caution and common sense when on the trails.

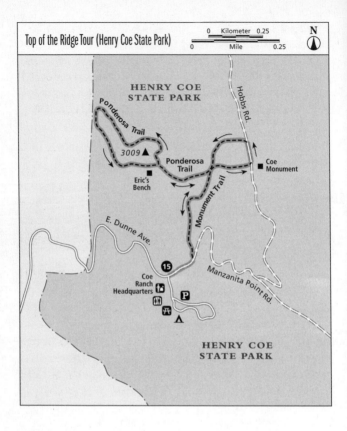

Top of the Ridge Tour (Henry Coe State Park)

0   Kilometer   0.25

0   Mile   0.25

N

HENRY COE STATE PARK

Ponderosa Trail

3009 ▲

Eric's Bench

Ponderosa Trail

Hobbs Rd.

Coe Monument

Monument Trail

E. Dunne Ave.

15

Coe Ranch Headquarters

P

Manzanita Point Rd.

HENRY COE STATE PARK

Other: Use restrooms at the trailhead and carry drinking water. Trailhead facilities include picnic sites, water, and trash and recycling receptacles. The visitor center, operated by the Pine Ridge Association, is open weekends and on Friday in spring and summer. Inside you'll find park maps, field guides, adventure packs for children, and other supplies. Park maps and other information are in outside displays when the center is closed.

Finding the trailhead: From U.S. Highway 101 in Morgan Hill, exit at East Dunne Avenue. Follow East Dunne Avenue east into the hills for 12 winding, scenic miles to the end of the road at the park visitor center and parking lots. The trailhead is at Manzanita Park Road, about 0.1 mile north of the closest parking space. *DeLorme Northern California Atlas & Gazetteer:* Page 116 C2. GPS: N37 11.245' W121 32.819'.

The Hike

I don't like to play favorites, but this hike rises to the top like cream, sweet on all the senses. It appeals to the mountain man (or woman), to the solitude seeker, to the armchair pioneer, to the vista lover. You'd expect to work hard for all these rewards, but that's not the case. It's quite simply a perfect day hike.

Let's start with the landscape. Climb to the top of the ridge through grasslands that whistle in the quiet wind and you'll find yourself in a ponderosa pine forest not unlike those that thrive in the Sierra Nevada. Press your nose to the bark of these trees and smell the vanilla, exotic in an area more typically permeated with the spice of bay laurel.

And then there are the views, which don't quit from trailhead to trail's end. When the weather is clear you can see south from the Monument Trail to Monterey Bay, north from the Ponderosa Trail to San Francisco Bay, and west from Hobbs Road across Middle Ridge to the Sierra. Fill the Santa Clara Valley with fog and the eastern valleys with mist, and you are alone on top of the world, civilization a thousand miles distant.

These landscapes and vistas are the legacy of Sada Coe and her father, the park's namesake and owner of the original Pine Ridge Ranch, Henry W. Coe Jr. The monument erected on Pine Ridge in honor of her father's memory captures the passion both felt for their beloved ranch. It reads:

May these quiet hills bring peace
to the souls of those who are seeking

The Coe family needed more than passion to manage their sprawling, mountainous enterprise. The notes of an "unknown ranch historian," printed on the park's official Web site, describes a life as much in the style of the Ohlone, the hunting and gathering natives who occupied the land before Europeans, as opposed to traditional ranching. Yes, cattle were milked and butter was churned and firewood was set up, but there were also wild berries to be gathered for preserves and deer to be hunted for meat. Even as the city grew up around it, the Coe ranch remained wild.

After her father's death in 1943, the ranch was sold to an outside company before Sada brought it back into the family. She ran the ranch briefly before donating it as parkland. Now it's part of the largest state park in northern California, and a delightful place to take a hike.

Options: In Coe Park, with more than 87,000 acres, a designated wilderness area, and more than 250 miles of hiking trails, the options are just about endless. Permits are required for backpacking, and reservations are required for car camping; visit the park's Web site for more information.

Miles and Directions

0.0 Start by heading up the paved Manzanita Point Road.

0.1 Pass a private residence to the gate across Manzanita Park Road. Take the signed singletrack Monument Trail, which heads uphill from the road, climbing through mingled oak woodland and singing grasslands.

0.4 Arrive at the Ponderosa Trail intersection in a saddle with great views. Go right (east) and up through the pines; you'll return via the middle trail, then loop out on the west section of the Ponderosa Trail on the return trip.

0.5 Meet Hobbs Road. Cross the road to the Coe Monument, protected behind a wrought-iron fence and depicting rancher Henry Coe on horseback. Return to the road and turn right (north) toward Frog Lake.

0.7 Arrive at the junction with the Monument Trail and turn left (west). The massive ponderosa pines along this brief stretch present the perfect opportunity to stop and sniff the bark.

0.8 Return to the Monument/Ponderosa Trail junction in the saddle. Turn right (west) on the Ponderosa Trail, ignoring side trails that break off into the brush.

1.0 The trail splits at Eric's Bench. You can take the loop in either direction, but the route is described going counter-clockwise. Views are fleeting through the pines, stretching east to the Sierra, and the walking is good, on a trail carpeted with pine needles. Fallen trunks are riddled with holes chipped by woodpeckers looking for yummy grubs.

1.3 Circle out of the forest and onto the grassland, where the views open over the San Francisco Bay.

1.4 Pass a picnic bench in the shade of a hammered old oak. You may not see them, but the quantity and variety of scat on the trail hints at the quantity and variety of wild creatures that live in the area.

1.6 Return to Eric's Bench, where you can rest and enjoy the vistas. Unless you want to do laps, retrace your steps back to the Monument/Ponderosa Trail intersection.

1.8 Turn right (south) on the Monument Trail and retrace your steps toward the trailhead, enjoying the views as you descend. They are like chocolate chips in a cookie—they melt you with pleasure . . .

2.3 Arrive back at the trailhead and parking area.

16 Chitactac Adams Heritage County Park

Short and charming, this interpretive trail through the site of an ancient Ohlone village opens a window into the lives of the prehistoric people that called this peaceful creekside site home.

Distance: 0.3-mile loop
Approximate hiking time: 30 minutes or more, depending on how long you linger at interpretive sites along the route
Difficulty: Easy
Trail surface: Crushed gravel, pavement. Portions are wheelchair accessible.
Best season: Year-round
Other trail users: None
Canine compatibility: Dogs not permitted
Fees and permits: None
Schedule: The park is open from 8:00 a.m. to sunset daily.
Maps: USGS Mount Madonna; Santa Clara County Park brochure and map to the park available at the trailhead and online

Trail contact: Santa Clara County Parks and Recreation Department, 298 Garden Hill Drive, Los Gatos, CA 95032-7699; (408) 355-2200; www.parkhere.org
Special considerations: Please leave historic artifacts and sites intact for the next visitor, including fragile petroglyphs. This is rattlesnake country, so use caution. No swimming is permitted in Uvas Creek.
Other: Trailhead amenities include an interpretive shelter, picnic tables, restrooms, water, trashcans, and handicapped parking spaces.

Finding the trailhead: From U.S. Highway 101 in Morgan Hill, take the Tennant Avenue exit. Head west on Tennant Avenue for 0.9 mile to Monterey Street. Turn left (south) on Monterey Street for 0.5 mile to

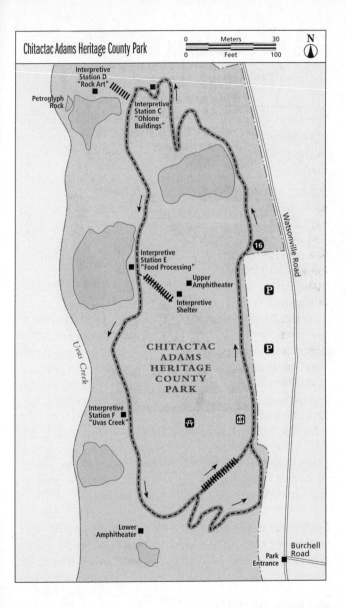

Chitactac Adams Heritage County Park

Meters 0 — 30
Feet 0 — 100

N

Interpretive Station D "Rock Art"

Petroglyph Rock

Interpretive Station C "Ohlone Buildings"

Interpretive Station E "Food Processing"

Upper Amphitheater

Interpretive Shelter

Uvas Creek

Watsonville Road

16

P

P

CHITACTAC ADAMS HERITAGE COUNTY PARK

Interpretive Station F "Uvas Creek"

Lower Amphitheater

Burchell Road

Park Entrance

Watsonville Road. Go right (southwest) on Watsonville Road for 5.4 miles to the park entrance on the left (west), opposite Burchell Road.

The Hike

So informative and lovely you'll want to do laps, the interpretive trail through Chitactac Adams Heritage County Park immerses visitors in the story of the Ohlone people and in the natural environment they occupied.

The trail is so short and well defined it's impossible to get lost, but it's so packed with information and beautiful scenery it deserves your undivided attention. Indeed, you may be so drawn in by the spectacular setting, with Uvas Creek pooling in a lush bottomland at the base of an impressive rock outcroppings, that you may miss fascinating details about how the Indians utilized the creek and the creatures and plants that thrive by it.

The panels in the interpretive shelter at the trailhead set the stage, revealing the complexity of the Ohlone culture that occupied the San Francisco Bay Area prior to contact with the Spanish. The panels, in both English and Spanish, describe the structure of native villages, from traditions and customs surrounding food preparation and social interactions to the materials and architectural design of village buildings. Medicine, basket weaving, and petroglyphs (symbols pecked and etched into rock faces) are described, along with the fate of the Ohlone after the arrival of Spanish colonizers in 1774 (perhaps earlier). The diversity of the culture is represented in the number of languages spoken by the related tribes—125 separate dialects were spoken by groups around the bay.

The trail begins adjacent to a huge polished rock outcropping where you'll find the first interpretive sign, about the village that was sited here. Settlement at Chitactac dates back nearly 3,000 years and likely included huts made of reeds or tree bark, granaries lined with bay for storing acorns, armadas for shade, roundhouses for gatherings, and sweat lodges for ritual use.

Switchback down into the riparian zone along the creek, where you'll find petroglyphs and the best kitchen on the planet, a cluster of mortars (grinding holes) worked into a sun-splashed rock outcropping overlooking the water. An enormous rock outcrop rises from a pool in the creek, where the Ohlone washed, caught fish, and gathered berries and medicinal plants. A grand old oak and another rock outcrop set the stage at the park's interpretive amphitheater at trail's end.

Focus on the Chitactac aspect of the park overshadows the Adams chapter, but a marker at the south end of the trail fills you in: In 1859 miner John Hicks Adams built the first of two schoolhouses on the site. The second schoolhouse stood here until it burned in 1956.

Miles and Directions

0.0 Start by passing the first interpretive sign and the huge rock outcrop at the north end of the parking lot.

0.1 Switchback down around the backside of the parking lot rock to the second interpretive sign on petroglyphs.

0.2 Pass the bedrock mortars. A staircase leads back up (left) to the interpretive center and down (right) to an overlook of the creekside pool where the villagers fished, washed, and harvested willow and berries.

0.3 Circle around an enormous oak and amphitheater, where interpretive signs describe roundhouses and the mission and rancho era. Look for petroglyphs on the backside of the rock that overlooks the creek. Climb back to the trailhead via either a staircase or a wheelchair-accessible ramp.

17 Miller Ruins Loop (Mount Madonna County Park)

A quiet forest of grand redwoods, scattered eucalyptus, and colorful acacia encases the ruins of the Miller family summer estate and the easy trails that surround them.

Distance: 1.4-mile loop

Approximate hiking time: 1 hour

Difficulty: Easy

Trail surface: Dirt roadways with short patches of pavement and a couple of short flights of stairs

Best season: Year-round

Other trail users: Equestrians

Canine compatibility: Leashed dogs permitted

Fees and permits: A $6 day-use fee is levied at the park entrance.

Schedule: The park is open daily from 8:00 a.m. to sunset.

Maps: USGS Mount Madonna; Santa Clara County Park brochure and map available at the trailhead and online

Trail contact: Santa Clara County Parks and Recreation Department, 298 Garden Hill Drive, Los Gatos, CA 95032-

7699; (408) 355-2200; www .parkhere.org

Special considerations: This is mountain lion country. An encounter is unlikely, but park managers have posted infor-mation signs advising how to behave should you meet a mountain lion while hiking.

Other: The trailhead area includes a ranger station, access to the Mount Madonna Bow-men's Club archery range, group picnic sites and trashcans, and horse hitches. Restrooms and a phone are located at the ranger station. Bring drinking water. Trails may be closed to eques-trians during the winter months; contact the trails hotline at (408) 355-2200 option 7 for current conditions.

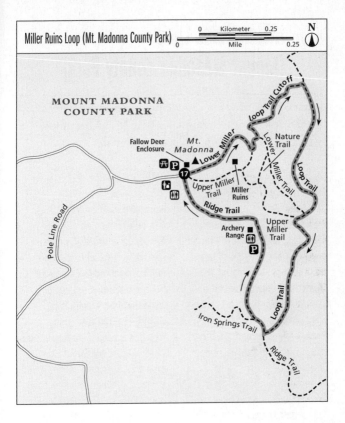

Miller Ruins Loop (Mt. Madonna County Park)

MOUNT MADONNA
COUNTY PARK

Fallow Deer
Enclosure

Mt. Madonna

17

Lower Miller

Upper Miller Trail

Miller Ruins

Ridge Trail

Archery Range

Upper Miller Trail

Loop Trail Cutoff

Nature Trail

Lower Miller Trail

Loop Trail

Loop Trail

Iron Springs Trail

Ridge Trail

Finding the trailhead: From U.S. Highway 101 in Morgan Hill, take the Tennant Avenue exit. Head west on Tennant Avenue for 0.9 mile to Monterey Street. Turn left (south) on Monterey Street for 0.5 mile to Watsonville Road. Go right (southwest) on Watsonville Road for 7.3 miles to Hecker Pass Road (Highway 152). Turn right (west) on Hecker Pass Road and go 5 miles to Pole Line Road and the park entrance. Turn right (north) on Pole Line Road and travel 0.5 mile to the fee station. Proceed past the fee station for about 1 mile to a Y and go right (north), through the gate toward the signed Henry Miller trailhead. The trailhead is at the end of the road, beyond the gate at the information billboard. *DeLorme Northern California Atlas & Gazetteer:* Page 116 D1. GPS: N37 00.723' W121 42.285'.

The Hike

Set on the crest of the Santa Cruz Mountains, enveloped in a deep forest that's cooling even in a hot spell, the ruins of the summer estate built by cattle magnate Henry Miller remain a great place to pass a vacation day.

Miller, a German immigrant who came to California hoping to strike it rich in the gold rush, instead made a fortune as a cattle rancher. A clever, enterprising businessman, he eventually amassed more than fourteen million acres of ranch land in California, Oregon, and Nevada, earning the title "Cattle King." He built a "bungalow"—pictures on interpretive signboards at the site of the estate show it to be rather more extensive than your typical country house— on the summit of Mount Madonna, overlooking the Santa Clara Valley. He and his family passed summers here, enjoying views that have been swallowed by a dense canopy of redwoods, pines, and eucalyptus.

The cattle baron died in 1916, and the state began purchasing land on Mount Madonna for a park in 1927. Today the park encompasses more than 3,600 acres, and miles of trails explore the redwood forest that dominates the heights.

The ruins of Miller's estate are the focus of a wonderful little nature trail that winds around a forested high point. Eighteen interpretive markers point out interesting remnants from the cattle baron's day, including acacia that blooms brilliantly in late winter, the estate's orchard and vineyards, and specimens of native tan oak and madrone (also called the refrigerator tree because of its cold bark). The route begins by exploring the ruins, then heads down concrete stairs into a more undisturbed woodland. Stands of majestic redwoods are sprinkled with impressively stout, white-barked eucalyptus that stand out like albinos. The redwoods don't take long to work their quieting magic, settling the most agitated hiker in a heartbeat or two.

The route eventually leaves the peace of the redwoods behind for an interesting climb through the park's archery range, where targets are set off the trail in the bush. Hikers can safely pass on the obvious Ridge Trail and may be treated to impressive displays by bowmen.

Miles and Directions

0.0 Start at the Lower Miller trailhead, pausing at the information sign that describes what you'll see along the nature trail.

0.1 Follow the paved trail down to the ruins and picnic area, all enclosed in a redwood grove. Interpretive markers lead the way through the estate grounds, and signs describe what you see.

0.2 Stairs lead down to a nature trail sign below the ruins. Go left (northwest and in the opposite direction from that indicated on the sign).

0.3 Arrive at the junction with the Loop Trail Cutoff. Turn right (north) on the cutoff, heading downhill through thick forest. Though you can't see the ocean, you can feel it in the air, which is moist even when the fog isn't in.

0.4 Reach the junction with the Loop Trail and turn right (southeast). Follow the old roadbed through the still redwood groves, first descending, then gently climbing.

0.7 Arrive at side-by-side junctions with the Lower and Upper Miller Trails. Stay left (southwest) on the Loop Trail at both, unless you'd like to shorten your hike, avoid the archery range, and explore the remainder of the nature trail by returning to the estate.

0.8 Pass an archery range sign that warns you to stay on designated trails. Pass through an area of thinning trees that permits glimpses down into the Santa Clara Valley to the left (east). The trail leaves the redwood forest and enters oak woodland and chaparral, where creosote bush warmed by the sun scents the air like chimney smoke. Look to the right (west) to spy a target (a deer) in the bush.

1.0 The Loop Trail ends on the Ridge Trail. Go right (north and up) on the Ridge Trail, a broad gravel road that leads into the woods. Watch for targets and archers as you climb.

1.1 Reach the junction with the Iron Springs Trail. Stay right (north and up) on the Ridge Trail (labeled Ridge Road on the park map). You're now in the archery range proper, with targets off the trail to the left and right.

1.2 Reach the parking area for the Mount Madonna Bowmen's Club, with restrooms, picnic areas, parking, trashcans, and of course, targets. Ridge Trail ends here. Continue straight (uphill) on Ridge Road. You may encounter auto traffic here.

1.3 Pass a gate, and enter a decidedly unnatural environment— the back side of the developed area around the trailhead— where you'll find Dumpsters, old tractor-trailers, and a radio tower. Climb past the park maintenance yard to the park road.

1.4 Visit the fallow deer—a gift of nonnative wildlife from newspaperman William Randolph Hearst that's kept separate from the resident deer population—before arriving back at the trailhead. (**Options:** Taking the Lower or Upper Miller Trail cutoff shortens the route to about 1 mile, depending on how you traverse the nature trail portion of the loop. You'll pass more remnants of the Miller estate on these trails.)

Trail Index

About the Author

Tracy Salcedo-Chourré has written more than a dozen guidebooks to destinations in Colorado and California, including *Hiking Lassen Volcanic National Park, Exploring California's Missions and Presidios, Exploring Point Reyes National Seashore and the Golden Gate National Recreation Area, Best Rail-Trails California*, and Best Easy Day Hikes guides to the San Francisco Bay Area, Denver, Boulder, Aspen, and Lake Tahoe. She is also an editor, teacher, and soccer mom—and still finds time to hike, cycle, swim, and walk the dog. She lives with her husband, three sons, and small menagerie of pets in California's Wine Country.

You can learn more about her by visiting her Web page at the FalconGuide site, www.falcon.com/user/172. Her guidebooks are available online through Falcon/The Globe Pequot Press, at various outdoor shops, and through local and national booksellers.

What's So Special about Unspoiled, Natural Places?

Beauty   Solitude   Wildness   Freedom   Quiet   Adventure
Serenity   Inspiration   Wonder   Excitement
Relaxation   Challenge

There's a lot to love about our treasured public lands, and the reasons are different for each of us. Whatever your reasons are, the national **Leave No Trace** education program will help you discover special outdoor places, enjoy them, and preserve them—today and for those who follow. By practicing and passing along these simple principles, you can help protect the special places you love from being loved to death.

The Principles of **Leave No Trace**

- Plan ahead and prepare
- Travel and camp on durable surfaces
- Dispose of waste properly
- Leave what you find
- Minimize campfire impacts
- Respect wildlife
- Be considerate of other visitors

Leave No Trace is a national nonprofit organization dedicated to teaching responsible outdoor recreation skills and ethics to everyone who enjoys spending time outdoors.

To learn more or to become a member, please visit us at www.LNT.org or call (800) 332-4100.

Leave No Trace, P.O. Box 997, Boulder, CO 80306

AMERICAN HIKING SOCIETY

Because you
hike.
We're with you
every step of the way

American Hiking Society gives voice to the more than 75 million Americans who hike and is the only national organization that promotes and protects foot trails, the natural areas that surround them, and the hiking experience. Our work is inspiring and challenging, and is built on three pillars:

Volunteerism and Stewardship

We organize and coordinate nationally recognized programs—including Volunteer Vacations, National Trails Day ®, and the National Trails Fund—that help keep our trails open, safe, and enjoyable.

Policy and Advocacy

We work with Congress and federal agencies to ensure funding for trails, the preservation of natural areas, and the protection of the hiking experience.

Outreach and Education

We expand and support the national constituency of hikers through outreach and education as well as partnerships with other recreation and conservation organizations.

Join us in our efforts. Become an American Hiking Society member today!

American
Hiking
Society

1422 Fenwick Lane · Silver Spring, MD 20910 · (800) 972-8608
www.AmericanHiking.org · info@AmericanHiking.org

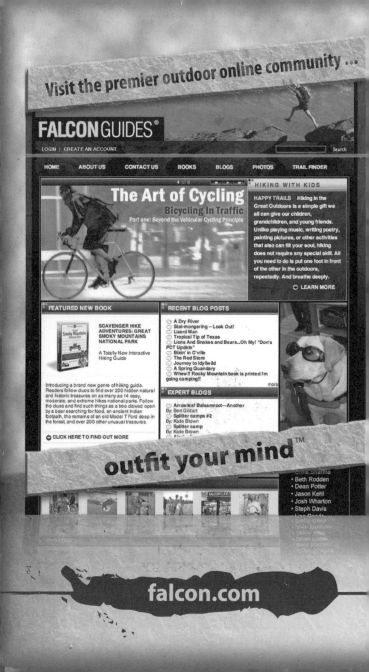